the *perfectly* roasted chicken

D0486766

H46 643 255 3

Mindy Fox

the *perfectly* roasted chicken

Photography by Ellen Silverman

Kyle Books

dedication

To my parents, Neil and Phyllis, and my brother, Jason, with love; your intuition, elegance and exuberance at the stove have long been an inspiration.

This paperback edition printed in 2013

First published in Great Britain in 2010 by
Kyle Books
67-69 Whitfield Street, London W1T 4HF
www.kylebooks.com

10 9 8 7 6 5 4 3 2 1

ISBN: 978-0-85783-210-8

All rights reserved. No reproduction, copy or transmission of this publication may be made without written permission. No paragraph of this publication may be reproduced, copied or transmitted save with written permission or in accordance with the provision of the Copyright Act 1956 (as amended). Any person who does any unauthorised act in relation to this publication may be liable to criminal prosecution and civil claims for damages.

Mindy Fox is hereby identified as the author of this work in accordance with Section 77 of the Copyright, Designs and Patents Act 1988.

Text © 2010 Mindy Fox
Photography © 2010 Ellen Silverman, except for
Book design © 2010 Kyle Cathie Limited

Editor Anja Schmidt
Angliciser Jo Richardson
Prop stylists Bette Blau and Deborah Williams
Food stylists Anne Disrude and Rebecca Jurkevich
Designer Carl Hodson
Photographer Ellen Silverman
Production Lisa Pinnell and Gemma John

A Cataloguing In Publication record for
this title is available from the British Library.

Colour reproduction by Sang Choy
Printed and bound by C & C Offset Printing Co.

Contents

INTRODUCTION

Here is a love story about chicken. Or perhaps it's a chicken story about love. It begins in 2002 on a sultry summer night in the deep South, when, chatting for hours around a hand-dug pit of slow-roasting pig, I fell for the affable gent who soon became my husband. It ends with the making of this book.

My sweet suitor was allergic to chicken; had been since he was a kid. A bit of a challenge, I thought. Still, it wasn't as if I had to keep kosher, go gluten-free, ditch all things dairy, or never crack a crustacean with my companion. As a freelance food writer and recipe developer, I couldn't altogether avoid preparing poultry at home but, save for a couple of slip-ups, I kept Steve free from the discomfort that accompanied his consumption of both the bird and its stock.

Then the cravings came. Unaware at first, I soon perceived a pattern. Every time Steve travelled out of town, I'd fix a dinner of roast chicken then savour the surplus over my next few meals, tossing the tender pull-apart meat, crisp salty-sweet skin, and rich natural juices into salads, soups, rice dishes and more. If my beau returned home before I'd had a chance to finish the bird, he'd gaze at it longingly and maybe try a taste to see if his sensitivity had dwindled. Sometimes it seemed as though it had, and then, well, maybe not.

Over a plate of pork buns, not long ago, my then new editor and I discussed the unparallelled pleasures of simple home cooking. The idea for this book took shape. On the subway back uptown, dreaming up dishes, I sadly realised an irony: for the next four months I'd be roasting busloads of birds, and poor Steve would enjoy nary a bite. My most valuable taster would be on an extended leave of absence.

Soon I was in the kitchen with a stack of raw chickens on one side of my cutting board and a blank notebook and pen on the other. I roasted the first bird. Bits of plump green olives, whole fennel seeds, fresh lemon zest and chopped thyme mingled under the skin as it crisped. Unable to resist, Steve covered a juicy shred of the rested meat with a spoonful of warm jus, and popped it into his mouth. Standing at the counter, he continued to consume until nearly half of the bird was gone, without a hint of adverse reaction. Stunned and optimistic, we considered the best: the allergy had run its course. A few birds later, our hunch

was confirmed. Steve had a new favourite dish, and I had my best critic back on my team. I couldn't have written the book you are holding in your hands without him.

Roasting chicken, like the cooking of most food, is very much about love. The simple dish is perfect for sharing and fairly certain to provide great happiness. One bird provides ample meat for a small group of friends or family. If you're eating solo, the leftovers make for delicious salads, sandwiches and more (it is helpful to know, as you cook through this book, that a roasted 1.8kg bird provides about 450g of shredded meat). And, for a party or larger crowd, or if you want to ensure leftovers, two or more birds can be cooked side by side.

When I figured out how many delicious dishes I could make with roast chicken (ones that made good sense with the bird included, not just tossed in willy-nilly), I couldn't decide which was more exciting – roasting the bird, or using the cooked meat to make tasty pastas; hearty soups; sandwiches à la Cuba and Vietnam; salads made with crimson blood oranges and crisp fennel, Serrano ham, hard-boiled eggs and green olives; salty smoked almonds and fresh figs, and so on.

Try any roast chicken you make, one with Indian seasonings, say, or a Greek sort, or a convenient store-bought rotisserie bird in any of the recipes in this book. Each bird will enhance the flavour of the other dishes a little differently and deliciously.

what makes a good bird, a good bird?

The best roast chicken you will ever make depends on three/four things: a good bird, good salt, proper seasoning.

'Good birds' include organic chickens, grass-fed and well-raised local types (from individual local farmers and family-farm brands). When you're shopping, always look for chicken labelled free-range, organic or RSPCA Freedom Food. However, be aware of what the labels actually mean as certain ones, like 'farm assured' can be found on standard intensively reared chicken and is no real seal of approval.

The multitude of labels at the supermarket can be confusing but the following definitions, defined at the time of writing, will help. Try several good birds and see which you prefer:

environmental benefits. Grass-fed birds can be cooked at the same temperature as their grain-fed counterparts but may cook faster, since they are leaner. Use an instant-read thermometer and begin checking 10 to 15 minutes earlier than the stated recipe time.

Raised without antibiotics: No antibiotics were used anytime during the raising of the bird, from pre-hatched eggs through processing. This does not mean the bird is organic.

Local: Local can mean within a county or region, or much closer. The essence of the term is three-fold: the product travelled a short distance from farm to table, thereby using minimal nonrenewable resources; purchasing the product supports a local economy and local farmland; and community is fostered between and among consumers and farmers. Local food can be organic but isn't necessarily so. Getting to know your farmer is the best way to understand how your food is being grown or raised.

Kosher: Raised and slaughtered according to Jewish dietary rules. Because the birds are hand-salted during processing, the meat is saltier than non-kosher birds. Use less salt to season before cooking.

Air chilled: A system that uses cold air, as opposed to water, to chill chickens during processing. Air-chilled processing is the norm in Europe and Canada but is fairly new to the US. Both processes have their own benefits.

Retained water: Chickens that are not air-chilled during processing are chilled in water, some of which is retained, and the amount must be declared on the label.

BUYER BEWARE/THINGS TO AVOID

Enhanced: A solution of water, salt and sodium phosphate that is added to the bird to flavour and tenderise it. The solution can increase sodium levels to well over 400 milligrams per serving – nearly one-third the daily recommended amount for most people. The solution also increases the weight of the bird, and thereby the cost to

GOOD BIRDS/ LOOK FOR THESE ATTRIBUTES

Organic: Raised without antibiotics and fed only organic feed (free from synthetic fertilisers or pesticides). The Soil Association Organic Standard provides the highest welfare levels in the UK e.g. smaller flock sizes for chickens. Freedom Food is the RSPCA's labelling and assurance scheme dedicated to improving welfare standards for farm animals. The scheme covers both indoor and outdoor rearing systems and ensures that greater space and bedding material are provided.

Grass-fed or pasture-raised: Raised on a nutrient-rich, low-fat diet of fresh and, in the winter months, stored grasses. Eating fresh grasses, on their own natural schedules, and spending much of their time outdoors, greatly reduces the need for antibiotics. Grass-fed meats are lean yet rich in 'good fat', including omega-3 fatty acids and CLAs (Conjugated Linoleic Acids), both of which are helpful defenses against cancer. Feeding animals on grass also has

the consumer. I recommend avoiding enhanced products, and using good salt to season on your own meat instead.

Natural, Free-range and Hormone-free: These three terms can be misleading.

Food labelled 'natural' does not contain any *artificial* ingredients, colouring ingredients or chemical preservatives and, in the case of meat and poultry, is minimally processed. However, meat from animals treated with artificial hormones, injected with saline solutions or containing 'natural flavour', such as processed proteins can also be dubbed 'natural'.

Free-range, though it implies the bird had access to the outdoors and consumed grass as part of a varied diet, does not have to be verified.

Hormone-free, especially seen alone on a label, can be used as an empty claim, since federal regulations prohibit any commercial grower from adding hormones or steroids to chicken products. None of these terms mean that the bird was not fed antibiotics.

the best pans and a few basic kitchen tools for roasting your bird

My favourite pans for roasting chicken are an enamelled cast-iron gratin (1^1/2- to 3-litre are a good size) and stainless steel or cast-iron frying pans (20- to 25-cm work well). A roasting tin is also good, especially if you are turning the bird while it roasts. But, generally, I prefer a pan with a lower edge to allow for more even heating on both the top and underside of the bird.

You don't need fancy tools to roast a great bird, just a few common ones:

An **oven thermometer** is important in ensuring that the temperature on the dial of the appliance matches the one inside the oven. Ovens often fall out of calibration and, if you do not know that your appliance is running under or over the temperature, you are liable to under- or over-cook your food.

A pair of **sharp kitchen scissors**, for spatchcocking, which is a fun term for butterflying.
A good **sharp chef's knife** (a 'good' one has a sharp, good-quality blade, is one that you like and fits comfortably in your hand).

A **chopping board**; **kitchen string** (tying the legs of a bird to roast is not a must, but it looks nice); a **wooden spoon** and a wad of **kitchen paper** help to turn a bird during roasting, if the recipe requires. Use kitchen paper to dry the bird before seasoning.

An **instant-read thermometer** for testing doneness.

Good salt and pepper.

salts and peppers: key seasoning tools

I generally use flaky medium-coarse salts – the kinds that crumble easily in your fingertips (as opposed to larger and harder coarse salts, which are best for a grinding mill) and fine sea salts for all of my cooking. Sel gris, fleur de sel and Maldon sea salt flakes and crystals are also terrific. Try various salts and see what you like best in both taste and texture.

For pepper, I purchase whole black peppercorns (buy them from a good purveyor to help ensure freshness) and I often tend to favour a very coarse grind, for the most distinctly peppery flavour. Most grinders don't do a coarse grind well, so I use the flat side of a chef's knife and a firm punch with the heel of my hand to smash the peppercorns into coarse pieces instead. Whole dried arbol chillies, Aleppo pepper (a sun-dried then ground red pepper grown in Syria and Turkey) and piment d'Espelette (a chilli from France's Basque region) are complex peppers that can be used in place of, or in tandem with, black peppercorns.

the beauty of the freezer for cooked chicken, bones and stocks

While writing this book, I discovered a newfound love for my freezer. As I roasted chickens, I froze the necks, backs (when the chickens were butterflied) and, after the cooked meat was eaten, the carcasses to use for delicious homemade stock. I froze the stock, as well as shreds of roast chicken, to use for rice dishes, pastas, soups and stews. I got everything I could from each and every bird, and it was all appreciated and enjoyed. Nothing was wasted. Using your freezer in this way is truly putting the philosophy of this book to work. Use resealable bags for chicken parts and carcasses, airtight containers (leaving a 2.5cm space at the top) for stock, and masking tape and a permanent marker to label and date items before freezing. It also helps to keep a list of what's in the freezer, to ensure items get used (See page 100 for more on homemade stock).

prepping the bird

Most of the recipes in this book call for whole birds, and there are some that require spatchcocked or butterflied birds, or whole birds cut into 10 pieces. Cutting up your own chicken is more economical than buying parts. You pay less per kilo, and you also get more meat per kilo, as precut meat is often poorly trimmed. There are many helpful visual resources on the Internet, should you need further help in spatchcocking or cutting up a whole bird.

To prep a whole bird: Remove the neck and giblets, then follow the recipe instructions, being sure to dry the bird well before seasoning.

To spatchcock or butterfly a bird: Use a good sharp pair of kitchen scissors to cut out the backbone by placing the chicken breast-side down, and cutting along one side of the backbone first, and then the other (use the backbone to make stock; see page 100). Turn the bird breast-side up and gently but firmly press between the breasts to break the breastbone and flatten the bird, then tuck the wings under.

To cut a whole chicken into 10 pieces: With the chicken breast-side up, pull one leg away from the body. Use a sharp chef's knife to cut between the thigh and the body, removing the leg. Repeat with the other leg. Put one chicken leg, skin-side down, on the chopping board and, slicing firmly, cut the leg between the drumstick and the thigh. Repeat with the other leg. With the bird still breast-side up, remove the wings by slicing away the wing from the inside, just over the joint. Cut the carcass lengthways into two halves – back portion and breast portion; cut the back portion crossways into two pieces, then cut the breast lengthways into two pieces.

resting, carving and gravy or jus

I like to roast a bird until an instant-read thermometer registers 74°C/165°F in the thickest part of the thigh, then let it rest for 10 minutes before carving (during which time the bird will cook a bit further).

To carve a roast bird, put the bird on a chopping board, breast-side up, and cut off a leg by slicing the skin between the leg and the breast, then following the curve of the leg around the backside of the bird. Repeat with the other leg, then cut the drumsticks from the thighs. Cut the breast down the middle and serve it on the bone, or cut the wings from the body of the bird and then, cutting along each side of the breastbone, cut and use your hand gently to pull the breasts from the carcass. The breasts, off the bone, can be cut crossways in half or into smaller pieces. Pull any delicious, tender meat from the bones and add them to your serving platter. Then... There are two succulent pieces of meat lodged in the backbone, called the 'oysters' – be sure to scoop these out with your fingers and eat them. The triangular tip at the base of the backbone is scrumptious, too. The carcass will make a fantastic stock, and can be used right away or frozen for such purposes.

I am not fancy when it comes to making gravy or sauces for roast birds. The pan juices created during roasting from the olive oil or butter, seasonings and natural chicken fat from the bird are so divine on their own that I generally prefer to simply stir them up and spoon them over the cooked meat.

Chapter one

ROASTING *the* BIRD

ROAST CHICKEN with BASIL, SPRING ONION, LEMON BUTTER and POTATOES

Serves 4

I'll never tire of a butter-rubbed chicken roasted with rich, earthy potatoes tucked along its edges. Still, it's nice to update the classic pairing with a simple tweak or two. Here, when the bird is almost done, I sprinkle whole parsley leaves and squeeze a few lemon quarters over the potatoes, then pop the whole thing back into the oven. The herb leaves crisp up and the lemon pieces caramelise. Some might find the lemon rinds intense, but if you like that sort of thing, you'll enjoy sliced bits of them with the rest of the dish.

1 x 1.8kg whole chicken

10g thinly sliced basil leaves

70g unsalted butter, at room temperature

2 lemons

5 garlic cloves, very thinly sliced

2 spring onions, very thinly sliced

flaky coarse sea salt

freshly cracked black pepper

800g small to medium potatoes
(about 4cm in diameter), cut lengthways into quarters

2 tablespoons extra-virgin olive oil

about ½ good-sized bunch of parsley, all but 2cm of stems removed

Preheat the oven to 230°C/Gas Mark 8 with the shelf in the middle. Pull off the excess fat around the cavity of the chicken and discard, then rinse and pat dry very well, inside and out. From the edge of the cavity, slip a finger under the skin of each breast, then gently but thoroughly loosen the skin from the meat of the breasts and thighs.

Put the basil and butter in a bowl. Finely zest the lemons into the bowl, holding the zester close so that you capture the flavourful oil that sprays from the lemons as you zest. Add the garlic and spring onions and mix to combine thoroughly.

Using your hands and working with about 15g of the butter mixture at a time, gently push the mixture into the space you created between the chicken skin and meat, being careful not to tear the skin. As you work the mixture in, gently rub your hand over the outside of the skin to smooth out the mixture and push it further down between the skin and meat where you may not be able to reach with your hand.

Season the chicken all over, using 2–3 teaspoons salt and a generous amount of pepper, then tie the legs together with kitchen string. In a large bowl, toss the potatoes with the oil, ½ teaspoon salt and a generous sprinkling of pepper to coat well. Cut 1 lemon into quarters and set aside.

Put a roasting tin (not non-stick) or 23 x 33cm baking dish in the oven to heat for 10 minutes. Remove the pan from the oven and immediately put the potatoes and any oil left in the bowl into the pan, keeping them in a single layer and pushed to the edges of the pan to make room for the chicken (it's fine if the bird sits on some of the potatoes); put the chicken into the pan, breast-side up.

your pick of potatoes

My favourite potatoes to use for this dish are a mix of farmer's market varieties, including Pink Fir Apple, Red Cara, Blue Danube, Yellow Bonnie and more. It's fine to purchase potatoes of different shapes and sizes - just be sure to cut them into roughly same-sized pieces so that they cook through at the same rate.

Roast for 20 minutes, then remove the tin from the oven and turn the chicken breast-side down. Continue to roast for a further 20 minutes, then remove the tin from the oven and turn the bird breast-side up again. Sprinkle the parsley over the potatoes, then stir the parsley and potatoes to coat with the pan juices. Squeeze 3 pieces of the cut lemon over the chicken and put the squeezed rinds into the roasting tin. Continue to roast for a further 20–30 minutes until the juices of the chicken run clear when the thigh is pierced with a fork, or when an instant-read thermometer inserted into the thickest part of the thigh reads 74°C.

Remove from the oven and leave the chicken to rest in the tin for 15 minutes, then transfer to a chopping board and carve. Spoon the pan juices over the chicken and serve with the potatoes and lemon pieces, if desired.

ROAST CHICKEN *with* GREEN OLIVES, FENNEL SEEDS *and* THYME

If an olive can 'make' a roast chicken, then this is the bird that proves it. Mild and fruity, there are two types of olives that work well in this dish, to blend with the floral flavours of fennel seed and thyme: France's prized Lucques (originally Italian, but now mainly cultivated in the Languedoc), and Cerignolas, from Apulia, Italy. Both are large, meaty, deliciously fruity sorts, with barely a hint of salt.

Serves 4

1 x 1.8kg whole chicken

about 10 green olives, preferably Lucques or Cerignola, stoned and finely chopped

2½ tablespoons finely chopped thyme leaves

1 garlic clove, thinly sliced

2 lemons

1¾ teaspoons fennel seeds

½ tablespoon flaky coarse sea salt, plus extra for serving

two ways to pit

To stone olives, use the side of a chef's knife, with the base of your palm on top, to press down on one olive at a time. Some stones will pop out of the flesh effortlessly. If they hold tight, use a sharp paring knife to cut the flesh away.

Preheat the oven to 230°C/Gas Mark 8.

Rinse the chicken and pat dry very well, inside and out. From the edge of the cavity, slip a finger under the skin of each breast, then gently but thoroughly use your fingers to loosen the skin from the meat of the breasts and thighs.

Mound the olives, thyme and garlic on your chopping board and zest the lemons right over the top of the mixture, holding the zester close to the mixture so that you capture the flavourful oil that sprays from the lemons as you zest. Chop the mixture together a little more, then mix in the fennel seeds.

Working with about 1 tablespoon of the olive mixture at a time, gently push the olive mixture into the pockets you created between the chicken skin and meat, being careful not to tear the skin. Once you have put the mixture into the pockets, gently rub your hand over the outside of the skin to smooth out the mixture and push it further down between the skin and meat where you may not be able to reach with your hand.

Put the chicken into a baking dish or cast-iron or ovenproof frying pan a little larger than the chicken and season with salt. Roast in the oven, rotating the pan once halfway through, for about 1–1¼ hours until the juices run clear when a thigh is pierced with a fork, or when an instant-read thermometer inserted into the thickest part of the thigh reads 74°C.

Remove from oven and leave the chicken to rest in the pan for 15 minutes, then baste with the pan juices.

Transfer the chicken to a chopping board; carve and serve with the pan juices and extra salt for sprinkling.

SEA SALT ROAST CHICKEN
with DELECTABLY CRISPY SKIN

Serves 4

Mixing up tasty butters, brines and rubs for roasted birds is a wonderful pursuit that rewards with tasty results. But there are times when the ease of a simpler recipe can't be beaten. Enter this no-fuss, crispy-skinned bird. The recipe is more technique-focused than ingredient-driven. No oil or butter is used – the skin crisps in its own fat with the aid of the salt, which provides flavour and reduces moisture. The key is to dry the bird very well before roasting; some like to air-dry the bird, loosely covered or uncovered, on a rack overnight in the refrigerator, but I find you can get a nice crispy skin without the overnight drying technique, as long as the bird is thoroughly dried with kitchen paper before it goes into the oven.

1 x 1.8kg whole chicken

4 short leafy fresh herb sprigs, such as rosemary, thyme and/or marjoram (optional)

flaky coarse sea salt

freshly ground black pepper

Preheat the oven to 230°C/Gas Mark 8 with the shelf in the middle. Pull off the excess fat around the cavity of the chicken and discard, then rinse and pat dry very well, inside and out. From the edge of the cavity, slip a finger under the skin of each breast, then use your fingers to gently but thoroughly loosen the skin from the meat of the breasts and thighs. Tuck the herb sprigs, or just the leaves from the stems, into the spaces you created, if using, being careful not to tear the skin.

Using 2 heaped tablespoons salt and generous pepper, season the bird all over, mostly on the outside.

Heat a 23–25cm cast-iron or ovenproof frying pan, or a 1.5–3 litre enamelled cast-iron gratin, in the oven for 15 minutes. Remove the hot pan from the oven, immediately put the chicken in the pan, breast-side up, and return to the oven (remember, the handle is hot).

Roast for 15 minutes, then reduce the oven temperature to 180°C/Gas Mark 4 and continue to roast, rotating the pan once halfway through, for a further 1–1¼ hours until the juices run clear when the thigh is pierced with a fork, or when an instant-read thermometer inserted into the thickest part of the thigh reads 74°C.

Remove the bird from the oven, sprinkle with a little more salt and leave to rest for 10 minutes, then transfer to a serving plate or chopping board. Spoon and discard the clear fat from the pan, leaving the juices behind. Spoon the pan juices over the bird to serve.

ROAST CHICKEN *with* MUSTARD BUTTER

Dijon mustard and a good slab of butter are staples in my fridge. Here, they work together nicely to flavour this classic bird. A simple sauté of mustard or other greens, and Scalloped Potatoes with Goat Gouda and Thyme (see page 47) make nice sides.

Serves 4

1 x 1.8kg whole chicken

55g unsalted butter, at room temperature

2 tablespoons finely chopped shallots

2 tablespoons Dijon mustard

2 tablespoons finely chopped fresh sage

1 lemon

flaky coarse sea salt

freshly ground black pepper

Preheat the oven to 230°C/Gas Mark 8 with the shelf in the middle. Pull off the excess fat around the cavity of the bird and discard, then rinse and pat dry very well, inside and out. From the edge of the cavity, slip a finger under the skin of each breast, then gently but thoroughly loosen the skin from the meat of the breasts and thighs.

Put the butter, shallots, mustard and sage in a bowl. Finely zest the lemon into the bowl, holding the zester close so that you capture the flavourful oil that sprays from the lemon as you zest. Mix all the ingredients together to combine thoroughly.

Using your hands and working with about 15g of the butter mixture at a time, gently push the mixture into the spaces you created between the chicken skin and meat, being careful not to tear the skin. As you work the mixture in, gently rub your hand over the outside of the skin to smooth out the mixture and push it further down between the skin and meat where you may not be able to reach with your hand.

Cut the lemon into quarters and stuff it into the cavity of the bird. Tie the legs together with kitchen string. Season the chicken all over, using 2–3 teaspoons salt and generous pepper.

Put a roasting tin (not non-stick) or 23 x 33cm baking dish in the oven to heat for 10 minutes. Carefully remove the tin from the oven and immediately put the chicken into the tin, breast-side up. Roast for 35 minutes, then rotate the tin and reduce the heat to 190°C/Gas Mark 5. Continue roasting, basting with the juices occasionally, for a further 25–35 minutes until the juices run clear when a thigh is pierced with a fork, or when an instant-read thermometer inserted into the thickest part of the thigh reads 74°C. Remove the bird from the oven and leave to rest in the tin for 15 minutes, then baste with the juices.

Transfer the chicken to a chopping board; carve and serve with the pan juices and extra salt for sprinkling.

DEVIL'S CHICKEN *with* SWEET PEPPER *and* ONIONS (ROAST CHICKEN DIAVOLO)

Serves 4

Diavolo means devil in Italian, which speaks to the peppery character of this tasty bird. The roasted peppers and onion provide a sweet counterbalance to the spice. Preparing the chicken in 'spatchcock' style (removing the backbone and then slightly flattening the bird) makes for quick cooking and easy carving, and offers a nice change of pace from a whole bird.

1 x 1.8kg chicken, backbone removed, breastbone cracked and legs slashed through the flesh in 3 places (see page 10)

1 lemon

2 tablespoons finely chopped rosemary, marjoram or oregano, or a combination

freshly ground black pepper

2 crumbled whole dried arbol chillies or ¾ teaspoon dried chilli flakes

flaky coarse sea salt

2 tablespoons plus 1 teaspoon extra-virgin olive oil, plus extra for oiling

2 red peppers, cut into 1-cm strips

1 large yellow onion, cut lengthways into 1-cm wedges, keeping the ends intact

125ml dry white wine

Preheat the oven to 230°C/Gas Mark 8 with the shelves positioned in the upper third and middle of the oven. Line a baking sheet with baking parchment.

Pull off the excess fat around the cavity of the chicken and discard. Rinse the chicken and pat dry all over very well. Lightly oil a 30cm heavy ovenproof frying pan (not non-stick) or large baking dish. Place the chicken, skin-side up, in the pan.

In a small bowl, zest the lemon and extract 1 tablespoon of juice. Stir together with the chopped herbs, 1 tablespoon of black pepper and chillies. Spread the mixture over the chicken and under the skin of the breasts. Season generously with salt and drizzle with the 1 teaspoon of oil.

Place the peppers and onions on the prepared baking sheet and drizzle with the remaining 2 tablespoons of oil. Using your hands, gently toss the vegetables to coat with oil, then arrange in a single layer. Season with salt and pepper.

Roast the chicken on the upper shelf and the vegetables on the middle shelf for 20 minutes. Add the wine to the pan with the chicken and continue roasting for a further 10 minutes. Remove both pans from the oven and, using a spatula or tongs, transfer the peppers and onions to the pan with the chicken, arranging the vegetables around the bird. Return the chicken to the oven and continue roasting for a further 20–25 minutes until the skin is golden and the chicken is cooked through.

Remove from the oven and leave to rest for 10–15 minutes, then transfer the chicken to a chopping board to carve. Serve with the peppers and onions, with the juices spooned over the top.

ROAST CHICKEN *in* PORCHETTATA

Serves 4

My friend chef Sara Jenkins inspires me in all things porchetta – fabulously aromatic, succulent, slow-roasted pig stuffed with a heady mixture of herbs and garlic – and so was the inspiration for this bird. At Sara's eponymous New York City shop, you can purchase her pork by the sandwich or plateful. In Italian, 'in Porchettata' means 'in the style of porchetta'. No, chicken is not pork. But this bird does right – and then some! – by its namesake cousin.

1 x 1.8kg whole chicken

55g unsalted butter, at room temperature

3 large garlic cloves, finely chopped

1½ tablespoons finely chopped fresh sage

1 tablespoon wild fennel pollen
(see Sources, page 172)

1 tablespoon finely chopped rosemary leaves

1 tablespoon finely chopped thyme leaves

flaky coarse sea salt

freshly cracked black pepper

Preheat the oven to 230°C/Gas Mark 8 with the shelf in the middle. Pull off the excess fat around the cavity of the chicken, then rinse and pat dry very well, inside and out. From the edge of the cavity, slip a finger under the skin of each breast, then gently but thoroughly use your fingers to loosen the skin from the meat of the breasts and thighs.

In a bowl, mix the butter, garlic, sage, fennel pollen, rosemary and thyme together well.

Using your hands and working with about 15g of the butter mixture at a time, gently push the mixture into the spaces you created between the chicken skin and meat, being careful not to tear the skin. As you work the mixture in, gently rub your hand over the outside of the skin to smooth out the mixture and push it further down between the skin and meat where you may not be able to reach with your hand. Tie the legs together with kitchen string. Season the chicken all over the outside, using 1 tablespoon of salt and generous pepper.

Put a roasting tin (not non-stick) or 23 x 33-cm baking dish in the oven to heat for 10 minutes. Remove from the oven and immediately put the chicken into the tin, breast-side up. Roast for 35 minutes, then rotate the tin and reduce the heat to 190°C/Gas Mark 5. Continue roasting, basting with the juices occasionally, for a further 25–35 minutes until the juices run clear when a thigh is pierced with a fork, or when an instant-read thermometer inserted into the thickest part of the thigh reads 74°C. Remove the bird from the oven and leave to rest in the tin for 15 minutes, then baste with the juices.

Transfer the chicken to a chopping board; carve and serve with the pan juices and extra salt for sprinkling.

MOORISH-*style* ROAST CHICKEN

Serves 4

Sometimes all it takes is a simple rounding up of basic storecupboard spices to give a bird a subtle yet complex flavour. In this case cumin, coriander and turmeric are blended with the lesser-known yet increasingly popular rich, smoky flavours of Pimentón de la Vera (Spanish smoked paprika). Pimentón de la Vera varies from sweet, 'dulce', to bittersweet and slightly spicy, 'agridulce', and spicy, 'picante', any one of which works well in this recipe.

1 x 1.8kg whole chicken

40g unsalted butter, at room temperature

¾ teaspoon ground cumin

½ teaspoon Pimentón de la Vera (see Sources, page 172)

¼ teaspoon turmeric

¼ teaspoon ground coriander

flaky coarse sea salt

freshly cracked black pepper

Preheat the oven to 230°C/Gas Mark 8 with the shelf in the middle. Pull off the excess fat around the cavity of the chicken and discard, then rinse and pat dry very well, inside and out. From the edge of the cavity, slip a finger under the skin of each breast, then gently but thoroughly loosen the skin from the meat of the breasts and thighs.

In a bowl, mix the butter, cumin, paprika, turmeric and coriander together well.

Using your hands and working with about 15g of the butter mixture at a time, gently push the mixture into the spaces you created between the chicken skin and meat, being careful not to tear the skin. As you work the mixture in, gently rub your hand over the outside of the skin to smooth out the mixture and push it further down between the skin and meat where you may not be able to reach with your hand. Tie together the legs with kitchen string. Season the chicken all over the outside, using 1 tablespoon of salt and generous pepper.

Put a roasting tin (not non-stick) or 23 x 33cm baking dish in the oven to heat for 10 minutes. Remove from the oven and immediately put the chicken into the pan, breast-side up. Roast for 15 minutes, then rotate the pan and reduce the heat to 180°C/Gas Mark 4. Continue roasting, basting with the juices occasionally, for about a further 1 hour until the juices run clear when the thigh is pierced with a fork, or when an instant-read thermometer inserted into the thickest part of the thigh reads 74°C. Remove from the oven and leave the chicken to rest in the tin for 15 minutes, then baste with the juices.

Transfer the chicken to a chopping board; carve and serve with the pan juices and extra salt for sprinkling.

GREEK ROAST CHICKEN *with* CAPER BUTTER, ROAST LEMONS *and* SKORDALIA

Mmmmmm. **Anything Greek is delectable to me, and especially with** *skordalia*, **the thick, somewhat tangy, garlic-heavy mash of potatoes (and sometimes nuts or bread) that is served as a condiment for meats, a spread for warm pitta bread and more. If you're not a garlic fan, you can make this chicken without its pungent accompaniment and be quite happy. Bites of the roasted, somewhat caramelised lemons can be eaten with the chicken and** *skordalia*, **rind and all. While their flavour is intense, those who like it will enjoy.**

Serves 4

1 x 1.8kg whole chicken

3 tablespoons capers, preferably salt-packed, rinsed and soaked in cold water for 10 minutes, then rinsed again

70g unsalted butter, at room temperature

2 lemons

1 tablespoon crumbled dried oregano, preferably Greek (see Sources, page 172)

flaky coarse sea salt

freshly cracked black pepper

pitta bread, for serving

SKORDALIA

225g Yukon Gold or Mayan Gold potatoes

3 garlic cloves, roughly chopped

¼ teaspoon fine sea salt

⅛ teaspoon freshly ground black pepper

2 tablespoons red wine vinegar

6 tablespoons extra-virgin olive oil

Preheat the oven to 230°C/Gas Mark 8, the shelf in the middle.

To make the *skordalia*, peel the potatoes and cut into 2.5cm cubes. In a 3-litre heavy saucepan, bring 1.2 litres of cold water to the boil. Simmer, partially covered, for 10–12 minutes until tender. Drain in a colander and leave to cool to room temperature. Push through a potato ricer or gently mash with a fork.

Meanwhile, prepare the chicken. Pull off the excess fat around the cavity of the chicken and discard, then rinse and pat dry very well, inside and out. From the edge of the cavity, slip a finger under the skin of each breast, then use your fingers to gently but thoroughly loosen the skin from the meat of the breasts and thighs.

Pat the capers dry, then roughly chop and put them in a bowl with the butter. Finely zest the lemons into the bowl, holding the zester close so that you capture the flavourful oil that sprays from the lemons as you zest. Add the oregano, then mix to thoroughly combine. Cut 1 lemon lengthways into quarters and set aside.

Using your hands and working with about 15g of the butter mixture at a time, gently push the mixture into the spaces you created between the chicken skin and meat, being careful not to tear the skin. As you work the mixture in, gently rub your hand over the outside of the skin to smooth out the mixture and push it further down between the skin and meat where you may not be able to reach with your hand. Season the chicken all over, using 2–3 teaspoons of salt and generous pepper, then tie the legs together with kitchen string.

Put a roasting tin (not non-stick) or 23 x 33cm baking dish in the oven to heat for 10 minutes. Remove and immediately place the chicken inside, breast-side up. Roast for 20 minutes, then turn breast-side down. After 10 minutes, squeeze half the juice from each lemon quarter over the chicken and drop the quarters into the pan. Continue to roast for a further 20–30 minutes until the juices of the chicken run clear when the thigh is pierced with a fork.

Remove from the oven and leave to rest for 15 minutes. Meanwhile, return to the skordalia. Use a mortar and pestle to pound the garlic and salt together to a paste. Transfer to a large wooden bowl. Add the potatoes and pepper. Using a large wooden spoon, pound the mixture together just to combine. Add the vinegar in a slow but steady stream, while still pounding, until incorporated. Repeat with the oil. Transfer to a serving bowl.

Carve the chicken on a chopping board. Serve with the pan juices, *skordalia*, lemons and pitta.

Note: *Skordalia* can be made up to 3 hours ahead and kept in a sealed container in the refrigerator. If the oil separates, stir together.

seek out salt-packed

When you have a choice, go for salt-packed capers over those jarred in vinegar. The salted type are plumper, meatier in texture and livelier in flavour than those brined in vinegar, which have a tinny, acidic taste that detracts from the main attraction.

POT-ROASTED CHICKEN *with* BACON, CELERIAC *and* ROSEMARY

Serves 4

A heavy casserole dish. Piney rosemary. Sweet celeriac. Salty-rich back bacon. Crushed juniper berries. Homemade stock. Calvados. A good chicken. This is my winter roast chicken mantra. Say it to yourself a few times, make it once or twice and it might become yours as well. Use a high-quality bird (see page 6); those with a solution added for flavour not only taste inferior, they dilute this bird's delicious juices.

1 x 1.8kg whole chicken

5 rashers thick-cut back bacon, cut crossways into 2.5cm pieces

675g celeriac, peeled and cut into 4–5cm chunks

flaky coarse sea salt

freshly ground black pepper

125ml Calvados

1 tablespoon rosemary leaves

½ teaspoon whole juniper berries, coarsely chopped

wrangling the root

Celeriac is very simple to cut. Slice off the top and bottom first, then, using a knife or vegetable peeler, cut away the skin and roots. Small, heavy roots offer a denser, more tender flesh than larger, lighter ones, which may have hollow spots inside. Be sure to cut celeriac to the size indicated; smaller pieces get mushy and larger ones won't cook through.

Preheat the oven to 190°C/Gas Mark 5 with the shelf in the middle. Pull off the excess fat around the cavity of the chicken and discard, then rinse and pat dry very well, inside and out. Tie the legs together with kitchen string.

Heat a 5.25–6.75 litre flameproof casserole dish over a medium heat. Add the bacon and cook for 3–4 minutes, stirring occasionally, until it releases some fat and begins to brown, then add the celeriac and cook for a further 5 minutes, stirring, until just lightly golden. Remove the bacon and celeriac from the casserole, leaving it on a medium heat.

Season the chicken generously on all sides with salt and pepper (about 1 tablespoon salt), then put the chicken, breast-side down, into the casserole. Reduce the heat to medium-low and cook, undisturbed, for about 5 minutes until the breast side is lightly golden.

Turn the chicken breast-side up, increase the heat to medium-high and cook for 1 minute. Add the Calvados and let it come to the boil, then carefully ignite with a kitchen match, keeping the lid of the casserole nearby to extinguish the flames, if necessary. When the flames die out, add 125ml water to the casserole. Return the bacon and celeriac to the casserole and sprinkle the top of the bird with the rosemary and juniper. Seal the casserole with foil, then fit the lid on well.

Roast the bird in the oven for 1 hour, then remove the casserole, uncover and leave the bird to rest for 15 minutes. Transfer to a chopping board, carve and serve with the celeriac, bacon, pan juices and flaky coarse sea salt for passing around the table.

MOROCCAN POUSSINS *with* M'HAMSA

Serves 4–6

This is a fun and slightly more formal bird than the others in this book. The ingredients require some effort to procure, yet are certainly worth it and can be modifed as follows. M'hamsa is a fantastic Tunisian hand-rolled, large-grain couscous with a toasted quality and a toothsome bite. Israeli couscous, which also has a large grain, and the more common and much smaller Moroccan couscous, can also be used in a similar fashion, though you may need to adjust cooking technique and timing accordingly. A sweet-tart blood orange is my preferred citrus for this dish, but when they're unavailable, I use a juice orange instead. The heat of harissa varies with the brand. Add a little more or less than I call for, as you like. If you're not a fan of coriander, parsley works well, too.

4 poussins (about 450g each), halved lengthways

24 stoned dry-cured black olives

85g unsalted butter, at room temperature

1 blood orange

75g plus 3 tablespoons finely chopped onion

2 teaspoons harissa

2 tablespoons finely chopped coriander, plus extra for sprinkling

fine sea salt

freshly ground black pepper

3 tablespoons extra-virgin olive oil, plus extra for drizzling

350g M'hamsa couscous

flaky coarse sea salt

Preheat the oven to 240°C/Gas Mark 9 with the shelf in the middle. Rinse the chicken pieces and pat dry very well on both sides. Use your fingers to gently loosen the skin from the meat.

Finely chop enough of the black olives to make 3 tablespoons; roughly chop the rest. Put the finely chopped olives and butter in a bowl. Finely zest the orange into the bowl, holding the zester close so that you capture the flavourful oil that sprays from the orange as you zest. Add the 3 tablespoons of onion to the bowl, the harissa and coriander; mix together to thoroughly combine. Into a separate bowl, squeeze the juice from the orange and set aside.

Spread the flavoured butter under the skin of the poussin halves, then pat the skin sides dry again and season well with salt and pepper.

Heat 1 tablespoon of the oil in a 30cm heavy frying pan over a medium-high heat until hot but not smoking. Reduce the heat to medium and cook 4 poussin halves, skin-side down, for about 6 minutes until golden. Transfer, skin-side up, to a large baking dish or baking tray. Repeat with the remaining halves, without adding more oil to the pan.

In a large saucepan, bring 700ml water to a simmer, then remove from the heat and cover to keep hot. Heat the remaining oil in a large flameproof casserole dish over a medium-high heat. Add the remaining onion, reduce the heat to low and cook for about 5 minutes, stirring occasionally, until softened. Add the couscous and cook for 3–5 minutes,

splitting hens

To split poussins in half, use a sharp pair of kitchen scissors or sharp knife. With the breast-side down on a chopping board, cut along either side of the backbone, cutting close to the backbone to avoid the meat, then cut through the breastbone.

stirring occasionally, until the couscous is lightly toasted and starts to make a popping sound. Add the simmered water, bring to the boil and remove the casserole from the heat. Cover and leave to stand for 10–12 minutes until the couscous is tender but still a little firm to the bite.

Meanwhile, roast the poussins for 13–15 minutes until cooked through. Add the orange juice and a generous pinch of coarse salt to the baking dish after removing the poussins to a platter; heat to a simmer over a high heat and cook for 1 minute, scraping up the residue on the bottom.

Fluff the couscous, drizzle with a little oil and season with coarse salt. Serve the poussins with the couscous and pan juices, sprinkled with the remaining chopped olives and coriander.

ROAST CHICKEN *with* CHORIZO-LIME BUTTER

~~~~~~

When you carve this succulent roast chicken, little pieces of chorizo from under the skin tumble onto the chopping board. Scoop them onto your serving plates, then bathe the bird and its bits with the rich, tangy pan juices.

Serves 4

1 x 1.8kg whole chicken

35g unsalted butter, at room temperature

1 lime

55g fresh, fully cooked chorizo sausage, cut into 3mm cubes

1 teaspoon dried oregano, preferably Greek

⅛ teaspoon cayenne pepper

1 small unpeeled onion, quartered

flaky coarse sea salt

freshly ground black pepper

125ml dry red wine

---

choosing chorizo

Although there are many different regional varieties available, all Spanish chorizo is made from pork and flavoured with smoked paprika. It can be smoked or unsmoked and mild or spicy. Some sasuages are flavoured with wine or garlic. Drier air-cured chorizos are best sliced and eaten as an appetiser like salami, while the smaller fresh sausages, which I have used here, are for cooking.

Preheat the oven to 220°C/Gas Mark 7 with the shelf in the middle. Pull off the excess fat around the cavity of the chicken and discard, then rinse and pat dry very well, inside and out. From the edge of the cavity, slip a finger under the skin of each breast, then gently but thoroughly loosen the skin from the meat of the breasts and thighs.

Put the butter in a bowl. Finely zest the lime into the bowl, holding the zester so that you capture the flavourful oil that sprays from the lime as you zest. Add the chorizo, oregano and cayenne and mix together to thoroughly combine. Cut the lime in half, then cut the halves into quarters; set aside.

Working with about 15g at a time, gently push the butter mixture into the spaces you made between the chicken skin and meat, being careful not to tear the skin. Gently rub your hand over the outside of the skin to smooth out the mixture and push it further down between the skin and meat where you may not be able to reach with your hand.

Stuff the cavity of the bird with the onion quarters and the lime pieces, then tie the legs together with kitchen string. Season the chicken all over, using 2–3 teaspoons salt and generous pepper.

Put a roasting tin (not non-stick) in the oven to heat for 10 minutes. Remove from the oven and immediately add the chicken, breast-side up.

Roast for 15 minutes, then reduce the heat to 180°C/Gas Mark 4 and roast for a further 15 minutes. Pour the wine over the chicken and continue to cook, basting with the juices every 20 minutes, for a further 1 hour until the juices run clear when thigh is pierced with a fork, or when an instant-read thermometer inserted into the thickest part of the thigh reads 74°C.

Remove the tin from oven and transfer the chicken to a chopping board to rest for 15 minutes. Meanwhile, tilt the pan, spoon the fat from the pan juices and discard. Serve the chicken with the pan juices.

BERBERE-SPICED ROAST CHICKEN

Berbere is a complex, spicy, slightly astringent and insanely delicious Ethiopian spice blend that includes chilli, cumin, coriander, ginger and ajowan. I like to play to its tangy quality in this recipe by adding lemon zest and juice.

1 large onion, peeled, keeping root end intact

2 lemons

1 x 1.8kg whole chicken

2 tablespoons extra-virgin olive oil

1 tablespoon Berbere spice (see Sources, page 172)

fine sea salt

freshly cracked black pepper

Preheat the oven to 220°C/Gas Mark 7 with the shelf in the middle. Cut the onion crossways into 1cm rings, keeping the slices intact. Lay the onion slices, overlapping if necessary, in the baking dish, frying pan or small roasting tin you are using to roast the chicken.

Finely zest the lemons into a bowl, holding the zester close so that you capture the flavourful oil that sprays from the lemons as you zest. Cut one lemon in half crossways, then one of the halves into quarters.

Pull off the excess fat around the cavity of the chicken and discard, then rinse and pat dry very well, inside and out. From the edge of the cavity, slip a finger under the skin of each breast, then gently but thoroughly loosen the skin from the meat of the breasts and thighs. Over the sink or a plate, rub the chicken with the quartered pieces of lemon, then put the pieces into the cavity of the bird.

Squeeze 1½ tablespoons of juice from the remaining lemons and add to the bowl with the zest. Add the oil and berbere spice; whisk to combine.

Put about 1 tablespoon of the spice mixture under the space you created between the chicken skin and meat of each breast, being careful not to tear the skin. As you work with the mixture, gently rub your hand over the outside of the skin to smooth out the mixture and push it further down between the skin and meat. Tie the legs together with kitchen string. Rub 1 tablespoon of the mixture onto the underside of the bird, then evenly rub the rest over the top. Season the chicken all over the outside, using 2 teaspoons of salt and generous pepper. Put the bird on top of the onion, breast-side up.

Roast for 15 minutes, then rotate the dish and reduce the heat to 180°C/ Gas Mark 4. Continue roasting, basting with the juices every 20 minutes, for about a further 1 hour until the juices run clear when the thigh is pierced with a fork, or when an instant-read thermometer inserted into the thickest part of the thigh reads 74°C. Remove from the oven and leave to rest in the dish for 15 minutes; baste again.

Transfer the bird to a chopping board; carve and serve with the pan juices and onions.

PERUVIAN ROAST CHICKEN
with AVOCADO SALAD

An enamelled cast-iron gratin dish or a heavy frying pan is a nice choice for this bird, so that after it's cooked the sauce can be made in the same pan. If you like, you can soak the red onion for the salad in an iced water bath for 10 minutes, then drain and pat dry before mixing with the rest of the ingredients. This takes away most of the bite.

Serves 4

1 x 1.8kg whole chicken

1 lemon, cut into quarters

5 garlic cloves, peeled

fine sea salt

3 tablespoons white wine vinegar

60ml plus 2 tablespoons white wine

2 tablespoons extra-virgin olive oil

2 tablespoons paprika

1½ tablespoons ground cumin

2 teaspoons freshly ground black pepper

½ teaspoon dried oregano

SALAD

2 avocados

½–¾ small red onion

20g coriander leaves

2 tablespoons lime juice (from 1 large lime)

2 tablespoons extra-virgin olive oil

flaky coarse sea salt

Pull off the excess fat around the cavity of the chicken and discard, then rinse and pat dry very well, inside and out. Over the sink or a plate, rub the chicken with 2 of the lemon quarters, reserving the remaining 2 quarters. From the edge of the cavity, slip a finger under the skin of each breast, then gently but thoroughly loosen the skin from the meat of the breasts and thighs.

Finely chop the garlic cloves, then, using the side and the blade of your knife, scrape and chop the garlic and ½ teaspoon of salt together into a paste. Working with a little of the paste at a time, gently push the mixture into the spaces you created between the chicken skin and meat, being careful not to tear the skin. As you work the mixture in, rub your hand over the outside of the skin to smooth out the paste and push it further down between the skin and meat where you may not be able to reach with your hand.

In a small bowl, whisk the vinegar, the 2 tablespoons of wine, oil, paprika, cumin, black pepper and oregano together. Put the chicken into a 3.75-litre resealable bag and pour the marinade on top. Pressing out the air, seal the bag, then turn several times to distribute the marinade around the bird. Put the bag into a bowl and refrigerate for 5–8 hours, turning the bag once or twice if you're home.

Preheat the oven to 220°C/Gas Mark 7 with the shelf in the middle. Transfer the chicken from the bag to a baking dish or heavy frying pan (see above) and pour the marinade into a small bowl (turn the bag inside out, if necessary, and scrape any thick bits of spices into the bowl with the marinade). Squeeze the remaining lemon pieces into the cavity of the bird, put the pieces into the cavity and tie the legs together with kitchen string. Season the chicken all over with 1 teaspoon of salt.

Roast the bird in the oven for 15 minutes, then baste with a little of the marinade. Reduce the heat to 190°C/Gas Mark 5 and continue to roast, basting every 20 minutes with the marinade and the pan juices, for about a further 1¼ hours until the juices of the chicken run clear when the thigh is pierced with a fork, or when an instant-read thermometer inserted into the thickest part of the thigh reads 74°C.

Remove from the oven and leave the chicken to rest in the dish while you prepare the salad.

Stone, peel and cube the avocados. Very thinly slice as much onion as you want to use. Put the avocado, onion, coriander, lime juice, oil and a generous pinch of salt in a bowl; set aside.

Transfer the chicken to a chopping board. Tip the dish so that you can see the oil separating from the pan juices; using a soup spoon, skim off and discard most of the oil. Bring the juices to a simmer over a medium-high heat. Add the remaining wine and, scraping any bits from the bottom and sides of the dish, simmer for 3 minutes.

Toss the salad together. Carve the bird, and serve with the pan sauce and the salad.

ROAST JERK CHICKEN
with PINEAPPLE MINT SALAD

Classic Jamaican roadside food, jerk chicken's warming sweet spices heat up cooler months, while its heat provides perfect picnic fare in balmy weather. Be sure to use good-quality olive oil and crunchy sea salt.

Serves 4

75g chopped white onion

5 spring onions, roughly chopped

3 garlic cloves, peeled

2.5-cm piece of fresh ginger, peeled

1 scotch bonnet or habanero chilli, stem discarded

2 tablespoons soy sauce

fine sea salt

1½ teaspoons ground allspice

1 teaspoon freshly ground black pepper

½ teaspoon ground cinnamon

¼ teaspoon ground cloves

¼ teaspoon freshly grated nutmeg

60ml extra-virgin olive oil, plus extra for oiling the rack

1 x 1.8kg whole chicken, cut into 10 pieces (see page 10)

2 tablespoons fresh lime juice, plus lime wedges for serving

SALAD

¾ teaspoon whole black peppercorns

1 x 1.3kg pineapple, cut into 2cm cubes

1 tablespoon plus 2 teaspoons extra-virgin olive oil

1 teaspoon flaky coarse sea salt

20–30 mint leaves

2 spring onions, thinly sliced on a long diagonal

In a food processor, purée the onion, spring onions, garlic, ginger, chilli, soy sauce, salt, allspice, black pepper, cinnamon, cloves and nutmeg until smooth. With the machine running, slowly add the oil.

Put the chicken into a 3.75-litre resealable bag and pour the marinade on top. Pressing out the air, seal the bag, then turn several times to distribute the marinade around the bird. Put the bag into a bowl and refrigerate for at least 2 hours or up to 1 day. Let the chicken stand at room temperature for 1 hour before cooking.

Heat the oven to 230°C/Gas Mark 8 with the shelf in the middle. Line a roasting tin with foil and add an oiled rack. Reserving the marinade, arrange the chicken pieces, skin-side up, in a single layer on the rack. Drizzle with the lime juice, season lightly with salt and spoon over the marinade. Roast for 50 minutes–1 hour until crisped on the edges and cooked through (tent with foil, if necessary, after 40 minutes).

Meanwhile, make the salad. Using a mortar and pestle or the heel of your hand on the flat side of a chef's knife, coarsely crack the peppercorns. In a bowl, combine the pineapple and oil. Crushing it with your fingers, add the salt, then add the pepper and toss to combine. Add the mint and spring onions and toss again; adjust the oil and seasoning, if necessary. Serve with the chicken.

hot, hot, hot

Like all ingredients, hot chillies can vary slightly, or more so, in intensity even among the same variety. So any recipe followed the same way twice is likely to vary then, too. The bulk of chilli heat is in the seeds. If you're after very hot spice, include more than one chilli, though you may want to leave the seeds out if you're using more than one. When handling spicy chillies, wear rubber surgical gloves and/or wash your hands very well afterwards. If you prefer milder dishes, make this dish with a less intense chilli or with none at all. The complexity of the dish is present, even without the heat

ROAST CHICKEN *with* SAFFRON, GINGER *and* SULTANAS

Can you assign a gender to a roast chicken? If the answer is yes, then this one is decidedly feminine. Its gorgeous floral aroma and flavour and pretty golden hue make it so. A simple plate of jasmine rice and lightly braised leeks make for equally graceful and delicious accompaniments.

Serves 4

1 x 1.8kg whole chicken

55g unsalted butter, at room temperature

1 orange

40g sultanas, soaked in boiling water to cover for 1 minute and drained

2 teaspoons grated fresh ginger

2 large garlic cloves, finely chopped

½ teaspoon saffron threads

½ teaspoon ground coriander

flaky coarse sea salt

freshly ground black pepper

225ml dry white wine

Preheat the oven to 220°C/Gas Mark 7 with the shelf in the middle of the oven.

Pull off the excess fat around the cavity of the chicken and discard, then rinse and pat dry very well, inside and out. From the edge of the cavity, slip a finger under the skin of each breast, then use your fingers to gently but thoroughly loosen the skin from the meat of the breasts and thighs.

Put the butter in a bowl. Finely zest the orange into the bowl, holding the zester close so that you capture the flavourful oil that sprays from the orange as you zest. Add the sultanas, ginger, garlic, saffron and coriander; mix together to thoroughly combine. Using your hands and working with about 15g of the butter mixture at a time, gently push the mixture into the spaces you created between the chicken skin and meat, being careful not to tear the skin. As you work the mixture in, gently rub your hand over the outside of the skin to smooth out the mixture and push it further down between the skin and meat where you may not be able to reach with your hand.

Tie the chicken legs together with kitchen string, then season the chicken all over with 1 tablespoon salt and generous pepper. Roast for 15 minutes, then pour the wine over the chicken, reduce the heat to 180°C/Gas Mark 4 and continue to roast, basting every 15 minutes, for about a further 1¼ hours until the juices run clear when the thigh is pierced with a fork, or when an instant-read thermometer inserted into the thickest part of the thigh reads 74°C. Serve with extra salt for sprinkling.

SWEET *and* SPICY KOREAN ROAST 'BBQ' CHICKEN

Serves 4

I dubbed this bird 'BBQ', in quotes, since the barbecuing isn't done in the traditional Korean way (with a soy sauce-based marinade called *bulgogi*). Instead, I mix up a sauce using *gochujang*, a thick spicy pepper paste, which tastes very 'BBQ' to me. Chicken wings work with this marinade, too. Use a 1.8kg chicken for this recipe.

125ml plus 2 tablespoons *gochujang* (Korean hot pepper paste), see Sources, page 172

100g granulated sugar

2 tablespoons sesame oil

1½ tablespoons soy sauce

1½ tablespoons finely chopped fresh ginger

1 x 1.8kg whole chicken, cut into 10 pieces (see page 10)

vegetable oil, for oiling the rack

flaky coarse sea salt

1 tablespoon sesame seeds

2 spring onions, trimmed and thinly sliced on a long diagonal

In a large bowl, whisk together the *gochujang*, sugar, oil, soy sauce and ginger. Transfer the marinade to a 3.75-litre resealable plastic bag. Add the chicken and seal the bag, pressing out the excess air. Turn the bag over several times to distribute the marinade, then put it in a bowl in the refrigerator, turning occasionally, for at least 12 hours or up to 1 day. Leave to stand at room temperature for 1 hour before cooking.

Preheat the oven to 220°C/Gas Mark 7 with the shelf in the middle. Line a roasting tin with foil and add an oiled rack. Reserving the marinade, arrange the chicken pieces, skin-side up, in a single layer on the rack. Season lightly with salt.

Roast the chicken for 20 minutes, then brush with some of the reserved marinade. Reduce the heat to 180°C/Gas Mark 4 and cook for a further 20 minutes. Brush with the remaining marinade and continue to cook the chicken, tenting with foil if the skin becomes too darkened, for a further 20 minutes.

While the chicken is cooking, heat the sesame seeds in a small frying pan over a low heat, shaking the pan back and forth, for 3–5 minutes until the seeds are lightly golden. Transfer to a plate. Sprinkle the cooked chicken with the toasted sesame seeds and spring onions to serve.

peeling, chopping and storing fresh ginger

Fresh ginger can be tricky to peel and chop. For easy peeling, use the tip of a small spoon, with the inside facing you, and pull it towards you. To chop, thinly slice the ginger, then stack the slices, cut them into thin matchsticks and chop. Wrap ginger in plastic and store it in a resealable airtight plastic bag for up to 3 weeks in the fridge or up to 2 months in the freezer.

TEA-BRINED FIVE-SPICE ROAST CHICKEN
with SPICY SESAME CUCUMBER

Serves 4

This lacquered-looking, smoke-kissed, subtly sweet bird involves a little advance planning but is otherwise easy and well worth the effort. The tea used is robust, smoky Lapsang Souchong; purchase it loose, if you can, since loose teas are generally better in quality than those in bags. A bowl of jasmine rice completes the meal. Save some leftover chicken to tuck into Chinese Roast Chicken Buns (see page 167).

1 orange

35g loose Lapsang Souchong or Russian Caravan tea, or 12 teabags

5 whole cloves

2 cinnamon sticks

2 whole star anise pods

1 teaspoon whole black peppercorns

1 teaspoon fennel seeds

3 slices fresh ginger (each about 4cm long and 3mm thick)

70g kosher or sea salt

50g soft dark brown sugar

1 x 1.8kg whole chicken

CUCUMBER

1 tablespoon sesame seeds

1 medium to large cucumber, preferably a skinny one

60ml toasted sesame oil

¼ teaspoon dried chilli flakes, plus extra for serving

¼ teaspoon fine sea salt, plus extra for serving

pinch of sugar

In a large saucepan, bring 2 litres water to the boil. Meanwhile, using a sharp peeler or knife, cut the zest from the orange, avoiding the white pith. If using loose tea, spoon into filters, or wrap in muslin and tie with kitchen string to secure.

When the water comes to the boil, remove the pan from the heat. Add the zest, tea, spices and ginger and leave the mixture to steep, uncovered and off the heat, for 20 minutes, then squeeze the liquid from the tea parcels or teabags and discard. Add the salt and sugar and stir to dissolve, then squeeze the juice from the orange into the mixture.

Pull off the excess fat around the cavity of the chicken and discard. Rinse the chicken and put it into a 3.75-litre resealable bag. Put the bag into a bowl, then pour the brine into the bag and seal the bag, pressing out any air. Put the bowl in the refrigerator and leave the chicken to stand in the brine, turning it a few times, for 12–24 hours (the more time you have to let it sit, the deeper the flavour).

Remove the chicken from the brine and pat dry very well, inside and out. Arrange a wire rack to fit over a pan, place the bird in the pan and refrigerate, uncovered, for 12–24 hours (you can skip this step, but it's well worth the advance planning – given the fact that the bird is quite wet from the brine, this step gives you the crispiest skin).

Heat the oven to 230°C/Gas Mark 8 with the shelf in the middle. Put a 20–25cm cast-iron frying pan or heavy roasting tin into the heated oven for 10 minutes. Meanwhile, remove the bird from the refrigerator and pat dry any dampness, inside and out.

Carefully remove the hot pan from the oven and immediately place the bird, breast-side up, into it and into the oven. Roast for 20 minutes, then turn the bird breast-side down. Roast for a further 20 minutes,

then turn the bird breast-side up again and continue to roast for about a further 20 minutes until the juices run clear when the thigh is pierced with a fork (1 hour in total). Leave the chicken to rest in the pan for 15 minutes.

While the bird is resting, prepare the cucumber. Heat the sesame seeds in a small frying pan over a low heat, shaking the pan back and forth occasionally, for about 4 minutes until the seeds turn a light golden brown. Remove the pan from the heat and leave to stand for a minute (the seeds will take on more colour). Transfer the seeds to a plate to cool.

Trim the cucumber at each end, then create stripes by peeling some skin off lengthways. Cut the cucumber crossways into 5-mm rounds. In a large bowl, whisk together the oil, chilli flakes, salt and sugar. Add the cucumber and toss evenly to coat. Use your hands to gently press each cucumber round into the pool of oil and spices in the bottom of the bowl so that each can pick up some of the salt. Transfer to a serving dish and use a spatula to drizzle all the oil mixture over the cucumber.

Using a mortar and pestle (or a spare pepper grinder), finely grind the sesame seeds. Sprinkle over the cucumbers, then sprinkle with salt and extra chilli flakes, if desired. Serve the cucumbers with the carved bird.

have on hand

Tea filters, or kitchen string and muslin for loose tea; a wire rack (a small rack is helpful so that you do not run into a space problem in the fridge) and a pan that will fit underneath it; a 3.75-litre reseable bag. A cast-iron frying pan is my pan of choice for this bird, but a heavy gratin, roasting tin, stainless steel or enamelled cast-iron frying pan work well, too.

TANDOORI-*style* ROAST CHICKEN

Serves 4

This chicken may not have the bright red hue you find in many Indian and Pakistani restaurant versions (the colour comes from spices or sometimes food colouring), but its flavour is tandoori all the way. The marinade works well on chicken wings, too. This bird requires high-heat cooking, so make sure that your oven is clean before you start, or you may wind up with a smoky kitchen. You could serve this with Freekeh with Onions and Olive Oil (see page 68), Green Rice (see page 50) or plain rice, Roasted Cauliflower with Dry-Cured Black Olives and Parsley Leaves (see page 63) or any kind of Indian side you like to make.

1 x 1.8kg chicken

175ml 0% or 2% natural Greek yogurt

60ml fresh lemon juice (from about 1½ lemons)

75g finely chopped white onion

4 garlic cloves, finely chopped

2 tablespoons peeled and grated fresh ginger

2 teaspoons paprika

1½ teaspoons ground cumin

¾ teaspoon ground coriander

½ teaspoon cayenne pepper

¼ teaspoon turmeric

1 tablespoon flaky coarse sea salt

olive oil, for oiling the rack

fine sea salt

Rinse the chicken under cold running water, then pat dry well. Cut into 10 pieces (see page 10), then make 5–3½-inch deep cuts in each piece. Put the chicken pieces into a 3.75-litre resealable plastic bag.

In a large bowl, whisk together all the remaining ingredients, except the oil and salt. Transfer the marinade to the bag with the chicken and seal the bag, pressing out the excess air. Turn the bag over several times to distribute the marinade, then put into a bowl and marinate, chilled, turning occasionally, for at least 6 hours or up to 1 day. Leave the chicken to stand at room temperature for 1 hour before cooking.

Preheat the oven to 230°C/Gas Mark 8 with an upper and lower shelf. Line a roasting tin with foil and add an oiled rack. One by one, transfer each chicken piece from the bag to the rack, skin-side up and in a single layer, letting any excess marinade drip back into the bag. Transfer the marinade to a bowl. Season the chicken with fine sea salt.

Put the tin on the lower shelf and roast the chicken for 20 minutes, then brush with the marinade, transfer the tin to the upper shelf and roast for a further 10 minutes. Switch the oven to the grill function, if you have that facility, or increase the temperature to 240°C/Gas Mark 9, and cook for 8–10 minutes until cooked through and golden.

Chapter two

WHAT'S *on the* SIDE

OLIVE OIL MASHED POTATOES with COARSE PEPPER and WISPY SPRING ONIONS

A forkful of juicy chicken and silky-smooth potato, swept through a pool of good olive oil, crunchy salt, coarse pepper and wisps of sliced spring onion, is heaven. A potato ricer (a handy tool that forces the cooked potato through a set of small holes, making it look like grains of rice) gives the mash a smooth texture. For a more rustic look and flavour, leave the skins on and mash with a fork instead.

Serves 4

1.1kg Yukon Gold or Mayan Gold potatoes, peeled and cut into 2.5cm chunks

flaky coarse sea salt

1 teaspoon whole black peppercorns

6–7 tablespoons good-quality extra-virgin olive oil, plus extra for drizzling

2 spring onions, very thinly sliced on a long diagonal

Put the potatoes and a pinch of salt in a large saucepan and fill with water. Bring the water to the boil and cook the potatoes for 12–15 minutes until tender.

Meanwhile, put the peppercorns on a chopping board. Place the flat side of the blade of a chef's knife on top and, using the base of your palm, press down firmly and a little to the side, to crush the peppercorns.

Drain the potatoes, then transfer them to a large bowl and immediately mash with a fork, or put them through a ricer. Stir in 1 tablespoon of salt, then, stirring until combined, drizzle in the oil. Serve warm with the spring onions, extra salt, pepper and an extra drizzle of oil on top.

oil for finishing

Higher-priced, good-quality extra-virgin olive oil is often referred to by chefs and food enthusiasts as 'finishing oil', because it's the type you finish a dish or dress a salad with. Good oil is a must for this recipe, since the flavour is a key component of the dish. Finishing oils are often marked with the name of an estate, a vintage and/or a 'use by' date, stamped on the label, bottle or bottleneck. Good-quality oils come from Italy, Spain, France, Greece, Morocco, South Africa, New Zealand, California, Chile and beyond. They range in flavour from piquant to mellow, and in colour from green to gold. I recommend tasting and storing one to three good oils, each with a different characteristic. Use them up within a few months after opening. Heat and light are foes to all oils, so avoid those in clear glass, and store in a cool, dark place.

ROASTED POTATOES *with* CRACKED PEPPER, FRESH OREGANO *and* GRANA PADANO CHEESE

Serves 4

Preheating a baking tray in the oven, then carefully spreading uncooked, olive oil-bathed potato wedges on the hot tin gives these spuds beautifully crispy edges.

900g medium Yukon Gold or Mayan Gold potatoes, cut lengthways into 1-cm wedges

3 tablespoons extra-virgin olive oil

1 teaspoon flaky coarse sea salt, plus extra for serving

55g (3mm) shards freshly grated Grana Padano or Parmigiano-Reggiano cheese

1½ tablespoons coarsely chopped oregano

½ teaspoon coarsely ground black peppercorns

Preheat the oven to 230°C/Gas Mark 8 with the shelf in the middle of the oven.

Heat a baking tray in the oven for 10 minutes. Meanwhile, in a large bowl, stir the potatoes, oil and salt together.

Using oven gloves (it's easy to forget that the tray is hot), remove the baking tray from the oven and immediately spread the potatoes and their oil in a single layer onto the tray; reserve the bowl.

Roast the potatoes for 20 minutes, then, using a metal spatula, loosen, stir and turn the potatoes once. Continue roasting for a further 10–15 minutes until golden and tender.

Remove from the oven and immediately transfer the potatoes to the reserved serving bowl. Add the cheese and oregano, tossing to combine. Add the pepper and more salt to taste.

SCALLOPED POTATOES with GOAT GOUDA and THYME

Serves 4 to 6

Variations on gratins seem endless, which is part of the fun of making them. Many gratins are made with double cream – tasty no doubt, but I prefer a lighter dish, so I use a mix of milk and chicken stock instead. You can try different cheeses, or use none at all; swap thyme for other herbs; use a mix of potato types, or play with other root vegetables, such as swede, celeriac or winter squash. If you're not using an unsalted homemade stock, use a low-sodium type and decrease the amount of salt in this recipe by half or two-thirds (you can always add salt to taste, once the gratin is cooked, but the problem of too much salt can't be reversed). I like to really taste the black pepper here, so I use a very coarse grind.

15g unsalted butter for greasing

85g goat's gouda cheese, freshly grated on the fine holes of a grater

900g Yukon Gold or Mayan Gold potatoes, cut crossways into 3mm-thick slices

3 sprigs fresh thyme leaves, stalks removed

1 small garlic clove, very thinly sliced

1½ teaspoons fine sea salt (use less if using store-bought stock – see above)

¾ teaspoon very coarsely ground black pepper

225ml full-fat milk

225ml chicken stock, preferably homemade (see page 98)

Preheat the oven to 200°C/Gas Mark 6. Butter a 2-litre gratin or an 28 x 18 x 5-cm glass baking dish. Set aside 25g of the cheese.

Arrange one-third of the potato slices in the bottom of the prepared dish, overlapping slightly and covering the bottom of the dish completely (you may have more than one layer). Sprinkle with one-third each of the remaining cheese, thyme, garlic, salt and pepper. Repeat the layering process twice more.

In a large bowl, whisk the milk and stock together. Pour the mixture over the potatoes. Put the dish on a baking tray and bake for 1 hour, then sprinkle with the reserved cheese and bake for a further 10–15 mintues until the potatoes are tender and the top is golden.

quick, even slicing

A mandolin-style adjustable-blade slicer is great for cutting potatoes and other root vegetables for gratins, and for making French fries and coleslaws. Inexpensive models can be found online and in some cook's shops. Most come with a safety guard, which should always be used. It takes a little longer, and pieces may be less uniform, but you can also slice the potatoes for this dish the old-fashioned way, using a good sharp knife.

POMMES FRITES *with* 3 MAYOS

A stack of crispy warm fries alongside a plateful of juicy roast chicken is one of life's great simple pleasures. Stir up your mayos first, to allow time for the flavours to blend. You can make all three, or prepare a double or triple batch of a single type. These are skinny, shoestring-style fries, which cook quickly and don't require a double fry.

GREEN GARLIC MAYO

½ teaspoon finely chopped garlic

generous pinch or 2 of fine sea salt

1 tablespoon finely chopped herbs, such as basil, parsley, tarragon, chives or chervil

3 tablespoons mayonnaise

SPICY MAYO

3 tablespoons mayonnaise

¼–½ teaspoon Sriracha or Asian Chilli Garlic Sauce (see Sources, page 172)

generous pinch or 2 of fine sea salt

SMOKED PAPRIKA MAYO

3 tablespoons mayonnaise

½ teaspoon fresh lemon juice

⅛ teaspoon Pimentón de la Vera (see Sources, page 172)

generous pinch or 2 of fine sea salt

FRITES

900g King Edward or Desiree potatoes, peeled, rinsed and dried

1 litre vegetable oil

flaky coarse sea salt

freshly ground pepper

To make the Green Garlic Mayo, use the flat side of your knife and the blade to alternately chop and gently scrape the garlic and salt together until you have a garlic paste. Stir the paste and herbs into the mayonnaise. Adjust the salt to taste.

To make the Spicy Mayo and the Smoked Paprika Mayo, in separate bowls, stir all the ingredients for each together. Cover all 3 mayos and refrigerate while you make the frites.

Using a hand-slicer or chef's knife, cut the potatoes into 3mm-thick slices. Pat the slices dry with kitchen paper, then cut them into 3mm-thick sticks. Cut the long sticks from the centre of the potato in half. Thoroughly pat the potato sticks dry.

Line a baking sheet with kitchen paper.

In a deep frying pan, heat the oil to 160°C, as measured with a deep-fat thermometer. In 5 batches, fry the potatoes for about 5 minutes per batch until lightly golden (return the oil to 160°C between batches). Transfer to the baking tray to drain. Season with salt and pepper and serve with the mayos.

> *have on hand*
>
> A deep-fat thermometer, for gauging the heat of the frying oil; a baking sheet and kitchen paper, for draining the fries; plenty of good salt and freshly ground pepper for seasoning.

GREEN RICE

Serves 4

Raised in New York and Chicago, I was a city girl until the age of 13. That's when my parents, en route back to their native east coast, chose country life in New Hampshire over a return to The Big Apple. Five acres of land complete with a small flock of sheep, a blackberry bramble, several rows of apple trees and a rope swing that dropped my brother and I into the cool of a well-shaded swimming pond on hot August days, replaced our suburban backyard grill and concrete pool. My mother planted rhubarb, blueberries and copious fresh herbs. Her gardens were among the first inspirations of what became our farm-to-table way of life and my fulfilling food-related career. This dish is dedicated to her. It's a nice way to use up an excess of leftover herbs from the fridge, or perfect if you have your own garden to snip from.

5 spring onions, trimmed

1½ tablespoons extra-virgin olive oil, plus extra for drizzling

1 large garlic clove, thinly sliced

200g jasmine rice

25g mixed chopped herbs, such as basil, tarragon, mint, coriander, chervil and/or chives

flaky coarse sea salt

freshly ground black pepper

½ lemon, cut into 2 pieces and pips discarded

Thinly slice the spring onions crossways, keeping the white and light green parts separate from the dark green parts.

Heat the oil in a medium saucepan over a medium heat. Add the white and light green parts of the spring onions and the garlic, reduce the heat to low and cook, stirring occasionally, for about 5 minutes until softened. Add the rice and 350ml water and cook according to the packet instructions until just tender and most of the liquid is absorbed.

Remove the rice from the heat, stir in the spring onion greens and herbs and season generously with salt and pepper. Drizzle with oil and squeeze the lemon over the top to taste.

POLENTA *with* TRUFFLED CHEESE

Serves 4

On the way to a friend's place for dinner early on New Year's Eve, Steve and I stopped to pick up cheeses and discovered Sottocenere, a full yet delicately flavoured truffled cheese from the northern Italian region of Veneto. Other truffled cheeses, or any semi-soft melting cheese like Fontina, can be used in its place. Don't skip the Parmigiano-Reggiano, though, which adds a required high note with its richness, tang and salt.

1 garlic clove, finely chopped

fine sea salt

185g polenta

140g Sottocenere or other semi-soft truffled cheese, or Fontina

40g freshly grated Parmigianno–Reggiano cheese

freshly ground black pepper

In a large, heavy saucepan, combine 1.3 litres water with the garlic and ¾ teaspoon of salt and bring to the boil over a high heat. In a slow, steady stream, whisk in the polenta. Reduce the heat to medium-low and simmer, stirring the polenta frequently with a long-handled wooden spoon, for about 20 minutes until it is thickened and creamy.

Stir in the cheeses and season with salt and pepper.

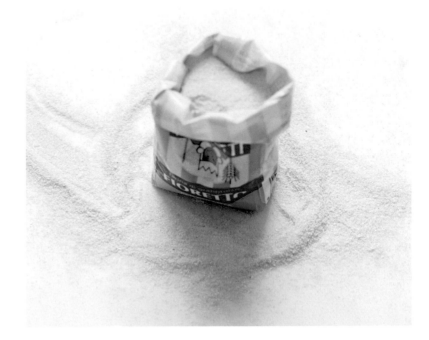

WILTED SPINACH *and* CHARD

Serves 4

A sauté of dark leafy greens is among the most beautiful and healthy of side dishes. This pure and simple version (sans garlic, chilli or lemon, though all are nice) allows the taste of the olive oil to be very present on the palate, which is the way I like it best. The oil and moisture from the greens create flavourful juices that blend nicely with a simple potato mash, if that happens to be on your plate, too. Use your favourite finishing oil (see box on page 45) for drizzling once you've taken the greens off the heat.

675g red Swiss chard (about 1 large bunch)

225–350g spinach (about 1 large bunch), tough stems and any wilted leaves discarded

60ml extra-virgin olive oil, plus extra for drizzling

flaky coarse sea salt

Cut the stems and centre ribs from the chard, discarding any tough portions, then cut the stems and ribs crossways into 2.5cm pieces. Roughly chop the chard leaves. Wash the chard and spinach and partially spin-dry, leaving some moisture on the leaves for cooking.

Heat the oil in a 4¾–5¾-litre flameproof casserole dish or heavy saucepan over a medium heat just until fragrant, then add the greens (in batches if necessary) and a generous pinch of salt. Cover and cook for 1 minute, then stir. Continue to cook, covered, stirring every minute or so, until wilted and tender, 3–4 minutes in total.

Transfer the greens to a serving plate and spoon some of the juices from the casserole over. Season lightly with salt and drizzle with oil.

WARM SUGAR SNAP PEAS *with* MINT

Serves 4

The simplest recipes are the best when it comes to understanding technique and ingredients. Here, the warmth of the just-cooked sugar snap peas releases the aroma and flavour of the olive oil. The peas are then cooled enough before adding the mint so that the mint leaves stay spry and bright. Choose a good olive oil for finishing (one you like the flavour of) and a flaky coarse sea salt (the one you love best for taste and texture). The special qualities of each ingredient are notable in the finished dish. You don't have to shell any of the peas, but the variety of shapes looks nice.

good basic kitchen salt, for the water

450g sugar snap peas, strings discarded

3 tablespoons good-quality extra-virgin olive oil

2 teaspoons flaky coarse sea salt, plus extra for serving

5g fresh mint leaves, preferably small and medium ones

Bring a medium saucepan of well-salted water to the boil. Add the sugar snap peas and cook for 1–2 minutes until just tender (the peas will continue to cook as they cool). Drain and transfer to a large bowl. Immediately add the oil and salt and toss to combine, then leave the peas to stand for a few minutes to cool.

Split 10–15 peapods, shell the peas and return the shelled peas and their pods to the bowl. Add half the mint leaves and toss to combine. Transfer to a serving bowl or plate, using a rubber spatula to get all of that good oil into the bowl.

Sprinkle with coarse sea salt and the remaining mint. Serve warm or at room temperature.

ASPARAGUS, MUSHROOMS *and* PEAS *with* LEMON *and* TARRAGON

Combining sweet asparagus and peas with the earthy flavour of mushrooms and the floral, liquorice notes of tarragon creates an interesting and delicious dish. A mix of mushrooms is nice, and you can use any cultivated or wild types you like. Mint or basil can be substituted for tarragon. I like the tender bite of not-too-done asparagus, so I give the spears a very quick cook in boiling water before they go into the frying pan. If you prefer them cooked more, boil for an extra 2 minutes or so.

Serves 4

450g asparagus, trimmed and cut crossways into thirds

good basic kitchen salt, for the water

2 tablespoons extra-virgin olive oil

25g unsalted butter

225g button mushrooms, trimmed and halved or quartered, if large

115g shiitake mushrooms (about 5 large), stems trimmed, caps halved or quartered, if large

flaky coarse sea salt

2 tablespoons finely chopped shallot (about 1 large)

115g fresh or frozen peas

finely grated zest of 1 lemon

2 teaspoons finely chopped tarragon

freshly coarsely ground black pepper

Cook the asparagus in a large saucepan of boiling salted water for 1 minute if the spears are skinny, or 2–4 minutes if they are a medium or fat thickness. Drain and run under cold water to prevent further cooking, then gently pat dry.

Heat the oil and half the butter in a large non-stick frying pan over a medium-high heat. Add the mushrooms and cook for 2–3 minutes until golden on the underside, then stir and cook for a further 1–2 minutes until golden all over but not softened. Transfer to a large serving bowl and sprinkle with a pinch of salt.

Add the remaining butter and shallot to the frying pan, then add the asparagus, peas and a generous pinch of salt. Return the pan to a medium-high heat and cook, tossing once or twice, for about 2 minutes until the vegetables are tender but still firm to the bite. Transfer the mixture to the bowl with the mushrooms. While the vegetables are hot, add the lemon zest and tarragon and toss to combine. Season with salt and pepper.

CORN ON THE COB *with* OLIVE OIL *and* CRACKED BLACK PEPPER

Serves 4

I've been slathering corn on the cob with good olive oil for years, all the while thinking my fondness for the pairing, though nice, was probably not worth a written recipe. Then one summer, when our friend Linda Wilkinson exclaimed that the duo was 'beyond', I promised the dish would make it into a cookbook one day. It works best when you use a good-quality finishing oil – whether fruity, grassy, peppery, subtle, assertive, that's up to you – and a liberal sprinkling of both crunchy sea salt and fresh coarse cracked pepper.

4 corn on the cobs, shucked

good basic kitchen salt, for the water

½–1 teaspoon black peppercorns

4–6 tablespoons good-quality extra-virgin olive oil

flaky coarse sea salt

Cook the corn cobs in a large saucepan of boiling salted water for 4–5 minutes until just tender.

Meanwhile, using a mortar or pestle or the heel of your hand on the side of a chef's knife, coarsely crack the peppercorns.

Using tongs, transfer the corn cobs to a platter. Immediately drizzle with the oil and sprinkle with salt and the pepper to taste. Serve the corn cobs warm or at room temperature.

---

salting the water

Save your speciality salts for sprinkling over cooked dishes and salads. For salting boiling water for pasta, corn and other vegetables, using a good basic kitchen salt, such as kosher, does the trick.

ROASTED RADICCHIO *and* ONIONS

A simple pairing of flavour opposites is often a big hit. Sweet onions are a perfect foil for pleasingly bitter radicchio, which, when roasted, becomes deliciously crisp at the edges. I love this dish warm, at room temperature and even cold, and I always make extra. The leftovers are fantastic warm with loosely scrambled eggs for brunch, layered on sandwiches or tossed into a pasta; they're also tasty enjoyed as a snack straight from the fridge.

2 medium heads radicchio (about 550g in total)

2 medium onions

6 tablespoons extra-virgin olive oil

coarse sea salt

freshly ground black pepper

Preheat the oven to 200°C/Gas Mark 6 with shelves in the middle and upper third. Line 2 baking sheets with baking parchment.

Cut each head of radicchio in half, then cut the halves into 6 wedges each, keeping the ends intact. Cut the onions in the same manner.

Arrange the radicchio wedges, cut-side down and overlapping slightly, on a baking sheet. Drizzle with 4 tablespoons of the oil and season with 1 teaspoon salt and generous pepper.

Arrange the onions, cut-side down, on another baking sheet in the centre (onions placed too close to the edges of the baking sheet may burn). Drizzle with the remaining oil and season with ¾ teaspoon of salt and generous pepper.

Roast, in the oven turning and swapping the baking sheets from the upper to middle shelves halfway through, for 30–35 minutes until the radicchio is browned and softened, with crisp edges, and the onions are golden and tender.

ROASTED PARSNIPS *with* ZA'ATAR *and* ALEPPO PEPPER

Serves 4

Za'atar and Aleppo pepper are extraordinary spices and worthy additions to the larder. Za'atar is a Lebanese blend of thyme, sesame seeds, sumac and salt. Aleppo pepper – a sweet-hot pepper grown in Syria and Turkey – is sun-dried and then ground. Sprinkle Aleppo on anything you want to add a little heat to. Both spices are great on everything from vegetables and pizzas to chicken, fish and more. If you're buying loose parsnips for this dish, choose ones that are similar in size. Small to medium are best for this cutting style, since they're more uniform in width than the large ones, which tend to have very fat tops and much skinnier tips.

2 teaspoons za'atar, plus extra for sprinkling (see Sources, page 172)

¼ teaspoon Aleppo pepper, plus extra for sprinkling (see Sources, page 172)

½ teaspoon coarse sea salt, plus extra for sprinkling

900g parsnips

2 tablespoons extra-virgin olive oil

Preheat the oven to 220°C/Gas Mark 7 with the shelf in the middle of the oven.

In a small bowl, mix together the za'atar, Aleppo pepper and salt.

Peel the parsnips, cut them in half lengthways (if you have very fat ones, cut them into quarters) and, in a bowl, toss them with the oil and the spice mixture to coat. Arrange the parsnips in a single layer on a baking tray. Roast for 20 minutes, then, using tongs or a spatula, turn and mix up the parsnips. Continue roasting for a further 10–15 minutes until golden and tender.

Remove from the oven, sprinkle with more of the spices and salt to taste and serve.

---

cutting long and slender parsnips

Cutting long vegetables (like parsnips and carrots) lengthways looks beautiful but can be awkward, depending on both the quality of your knife and the shape of the particular vegetable. To keep it beautiful, safe and easy, use a well-sharpened knife and, instead of trying to cut the entire length of the vegetable in one fell swoop, hold the knife in line with the parsnip and cut from the middle to the fatter end first, then turn the vegetable and cut from the middle to the skinny end.

GIGANTE BEANS *with* KALE

Canned beans simply don't come close in flavour to dried. Inexpensive and easy to cook, dried beans do require a soak, but once they're on the hob, they are virtually fuss-free. Make this recipe a day or two ahead, if you can, as the flavours deepen markedly over time. Leftovers can be eaten with their cooking liquid as a soup, mashed and then spread onto crusty bread or spooned alongside browned sausages.

Serves 4 to 6

450g dried fagioli gigante beans
(see Box below)

1 head garlic, unpeeled

2 large leafy sprigs of fresh sage or
rosemary, or a combination

1 crumbled dried arbol chilli
or ¼ teaspoon dried chilli flakes
or ½ teaspoon black peppercorns

225g (1 bunch) kale, stems and centre ribs
discarded and leaves coarsely chopped

coarse sea salt

extra-virgin olive oil, for drizzling

freshly ground black pepper

Rinse the beans. Wrap the garlic, sage and chilli in muslin and tie with kitchen string. Place in a large saucepan, add the beans and cover with cold water by 7.5cm. Soak for 8 hours or overnight.

Place the pan over a medium heat and bring to a simmer, then reduce to a very gentle simmer and cook the beans, adding water as needed to keep the water level about 5cm above the beans, for 1½–2 hours until the beans are tender. (If you're not serving right away, let the beans cool down in their liquid, then put the beans and their liquor into an airtight container and refrigerate. The beans and their liquor can be reheated over a medium heat.)

In small handfuls, gently stir the kale into the beans, adding more greens once the previous addition is wilted (add water as needed to keep the level just above the greens and beans). Once all the kale is in the pan, add water as necessary, to just cover the greens and beans, and 2 teaspoons salt. Return the liquid to a simmer and cook for 5–8 minutes until the kale is tender, then remove and discard the sachet of aromatics.

To serve, transfer to a serving bowl using a slotted spoon. Add a few splashes of the bean liquor, a generous drizzle of good olive oil and a sprinkle of salt and pepper.

---

key to good bean cookery

The most important thing to understand when it comes to beans is that age determines cooking time. The older the beans, the longer they will take to cook. Though it can be hard to determine the age of the beans you buy, even older beans won't cause a problem once you get into the kitchen. If the beans are not ready after an hour or so, keep cooking, adding more water as necessary, until they are tender. To get the best-quality beans available, look for those with a 'use by' date, and/or purchase from a reputable shop that moves product quickly (see Sources, page 172).

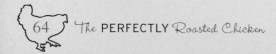

ROASTED CAULIFLOWER *with* DRY-CURED BLACK OLIVES *and* PARSLEY LEAVES

Sweet roasted cauliflower, salty, earthy olives and bitter parsley create a nice play of both colour and flavour in this dish. The core of the cauliflower is edible. Instead of tossing it, trim it, then cut it into pieces, similar in size to the florets. As is often my preference, I like to coarsely grind my pepper here, but you can grind it whatever way you like.

Serves 4

1 large head cauliflower (1.1–1.3kg)

75ml extra-virgin olive oil

¼ teaspoon flaky coarse sea salt

Aleppo pepper or freshly ground black pepper, or a combination

30g flat-leaf parsley leaves, washed and patted dry

50g roughly chopped, stoned dry-cured black olives

Preheat the oven to 200°C/Gas Mark 6 with the shelf in the middle. Line a baking tray with baking parchment.

Cut the cauliflower into 4cm-wide florets; cut the core into equal-sized pieces. Toss with the oil, salt and a generous pinch of pepper in a large bowl. Spread in a single layer on the prepared baking tray. Roast, stirring and turning pieces over occasionally, for 40–45 minutes until golden and tender.

Meanwhile, combine the parsley and olives in a large serving bowl.

Remove the baking tray from the oven and, while the cauliflower is hot, transfer to the bowl with the parsley and olives. Toss to combine and season with pepper to taste.

FARRO *with* SPICY SUN-DRIED TOMATOES *and* FETA CHEESE

Serves 4

Farro is a nutrient-rich grain, related to spelt. Its rich, nutty taste and toothsome texture is perfect for side dishes, salads and risottos (or 'farrotos', see page 130). Some recipes soak the grain before cooking it, and others require a much longer cooking time. The easy, non-soak cooking method here is the one I've always used (whether the farro is pearled, meaning the hull has been removed, or not, which may require a few more minutes of cooking time). This quick recipe also uses a favourite storecupboard item: spicy Tunisian sun-dried tomato spread.

good basic kitchen salt, for the water

280g dried farro

3 tablespoons good-quality extra-virgin olive oil

1 lemon

70g sheep's milk feta cheese, crumbled

1–2 tablespoons spicy sun-dried tomato spread (see Sources, page 172)

10g roughly chopped flat-leaf parsley

flaky coarse sea salt

Bring a medium saucepan of salted water to the boil. Add the farro and cook for about 18 minutes until tender but still firm to the bite. Drain and transfer to a bowl.

Add the oil, then finely grate the zest from the lemon into the bowl, holding the zester close to catch any sprinkles of juice. Toss to combine.

Add the cheese, 1 tablespoon sun-dried tomato spread, parsley and a few generous pinches of salt. Stir to combine. Allow the flavours to meld for a couple of minutes, then taste and adjust the amounts of sun-dried tomato spread and salt to your liking.

Serve warm or at room temperature.

make your own spicy sun-dried tomato spread

Les Moulins Mahjoub spicy sun-dried tomato spread is a blend of sun-dried tomatoes, olive oil, piment D'Espelette (a French chilli, widely used in Basque kitchens), garlic and coriander. If you want to make your own similar spread, you can finely chop and mix together the ingredients above, seasoning with salt and pepper, or substitute ingredients, using any fresh or dried chilli you like, and one or a mix of fresh herbs. If you are using sun-dried tomatoes that do not come packed in oil, then stir the paste together with good-quality extra-virgin olive oil to moisten. For those that do come packed in oil, drain them first, then use a good-quality oil in your mix, if extra moistening is required.

ROASTED RED and GOLDEN BEETS with BASIL

Oh, it makes me sad to hear people say they 'hate' beetroot. Beets are candy-sweet, gorgeous deliciousness. The matter of liking them is often more a matter of understanding how to prepare them than anything else. Using both red and golden beetroot bring added colour to the table, but you can make this dish with a single variety, depending on your whim or what's available.

Serves 4 to 6

900g red and golden beetroot (about 8 medium), trimmed, leaving about 5mm of the stem

6 tablespoons red wine vinegar

flaky coarse sea salt

freshly ground black pepper, fairly coarse

pinch of sugar (optional)

5 tablespoons extra-virgin olive oil

leaves from 1 small bunch of basil

Preheat the oven to 200°C/Gas Mark 6.

Put the beetroot in a baking dish and add water to come about 1cm up the sides. Cover the baking dish tightly with foil and roast the beets for 45 minutes to 1 hour or more, depending on size, until they can be easily pierced through to the centre with a knife or skewer. Uncover and allow the beetroot to cool.

Trim and discard the beetroot tops and tails, then peel the beetroot. Cut the red beetroot into halves, quarters or sixths, depending on their size, and transfer to a bowl. Do the same with the orange beetroot, putting it into a separate bowl (otherwise the colours will bleed). Add 1 tablespoon of vinegar to each bowl and a generous pinch of salt and pepper. If the beetroot are at all bitter, add a pinch of sugar. Toss to combine and let the beetroot absorb the vinegar for 10 minutes.

In a bowl, whisk together the remaining vinegar and the oil. Transfer the beetroot onto plates and spoon the dressing over the top. Arrange the basil leaves on the plates. Season generously with salt.

FREEKEH *with* ONIONS *and* OLIVE OIL

I recently discovered freekeh (pronounced 'free-ka'), a nutrient-rich, ancient rice-like grain at my local farmer's market. The first time I made it, I loved its nutty and somewhat smoky flavour so much, I heated up the leftovers for both breakfast and lunch every day afterwards until I had eaten it all up. This is a versatile side dish that works well with a range of flavours and can be used as the base for a freekeh salad.

150g freekeh (see Sources, page 172)

flaky coarse sea salt

4 tablespoons extra-virgin olive oil

110g coarsely chopped onion

1 garlic clove, thinly sliced

Aleppo pepper or freshly ground black pepper

In a medium saucepan, add 1.5 litres water together with the freekeh, 1 teaspoon of salt and 1 tablespoon of the oil. Bring to the boil over a high heat, then reduce to a gentle simmer and cook, covered, for 40–45 minutes until the freekeh is tender but still firm to the bite and the water is mostly absorbed.

Meanwhile, in a small saucepan, combine the remaining oil, onion, garlic and a pinch of salt and pepper. Heat over a low heat just until warm and fragrant, then remove from heat and set aside.

When the freekeh is ready, gently reheat the oil mixture, just to warm through, then stir the pan contents into the freekeh to combine. Adjust the salt and pepper to taste. Serve warm or at room temperature.

GREEK LENTIL *and* RICE PILAF

Serves 4

This delicious Greek side makes a nice twosome with chicken, whether your bird is cooked in a Greek style or not. Use small lentils like French le Puy, Spanish pardina, Italian castellucio or colfiorito – these types are firm-tender, not mushy, and hold their shape once cooked. If you have fresh parsley, coriander or chives on hand, a sprinkle just before serving lends a nice extra touch. A dollop of Greek yogurt on top is tasty, too.

200g small green or brown lentils, sorted of debris and rinsed

60ml extra-virgin olive oil

1 large onion, finely chopped

2 large garlic cloves, finely chopped

1 tablespoon dried oregano, preferably Greek (see Sources, page 172)

2 teaspoons ground coriander

½ teaspoon ground allspice

150g jasmine rice

1 tablespoon honey

1 tablespoon red wine vinegar

2½ teaspoons fine sea salt

freshly ground black pepper

Greek yogurt, for serving (optional)

Bring the lentils and 600ml water to the boil in a medium saucepan. Cover, reduce the heat to low and simmer, stirring occasionally, for 20–25 minutes until the lentils are tender yet still firm to the bite. Drain and spread on a plate to cool.

Heat the oil in a 30cm frying pan over a medium-high heat. Add the onion, garlic, oregano, coriander and allspice. Reduce the heat to medium and cook, stirring occasionally, for about 7 minutes until softened. Add the rice and cook, stirring, for about a further 2 minutes until the rice is toasted and looks opaque.

Stir in 400ml water and salt, bring to the boil, then cover and simmer, stirring occasionally, for 13–15 minutes until the rice is tender and the liquid is absorbed.

Meanwhile, whisk the honey and vinegar together.

When the rice is cooked, stir in the lentils, honey mixture and salt; cook for a further 1 minute. Season generously with pepper and then serve with yogurt, if desired.

Chapter three

ROAST CHICKEN SALADS

LITTLE GEM, SWEET TURNIP, ROAST CHICKEN *and* LEMON SALAD

Serves 4

Baby turnips are sweet, crisp, mild white beauties that are delicious raw in salads, or quickly sautéed or blanched. Their tender greens are terrific cooked in a frying pan with a little olive oil, for a side dish or to toss into rice dishes or pastas. No need to peel the little bulbs – just rinse, wipe dry and eat.

350g Little Gem lettuce (about 2 heads), leaves separated, torn if large

1 bunch of baby turnips, trimmed and cut into halves, quarters or sixths, depending on size

3 tablespoons good-quality extra-virgin olive oil

juice of ½ lemon

flaky coarse sea salt

225g sliced roast chicken

10–12 chives, cut into 4–5-cm lengths

freshly cracked black pepper

Toss together the lettuce, turnips, oil, lemon juice and a generous pinch or two of salt in a large bowl.

Transfer the salad to a serving platter or onto individual plates. Tuck the chicken slices between the leaves. Drizzle the chicken with a little oil, then sprinkle the whole salad with more salt, the chives and pepper to taste.

---

little gems

Little Gem lettuces are a small form of Cos, or Romaine, lettuce, with tightly packed heads and sweet, crisp leaves. Look for young, bright green heads, avoiding any that appear more mature, since these can be bitter-tasting.

WINTER ROAST CHICKEN SALAD *with* FENNEL, BLOOD ORANGE *and* PISTACHIO

Serves 4

This salad is evidence that beauty and simplicity can come together on a plate in a matter of minutes. This dish is best with a tart-sweet citrus; if blood oranges aren't available, try red naval oranges or pink grapefruit instead.

3 blood oranges

2 medium fennel bulbs, trimmed and fronds reserved

225g medium shreds roast chicken

3½ tablespoons red wine vinegar

3 tablespoons good-quality extra-virgin olive oil

flaky coarse sea salt

3 tablespoons shelled unsalted pistachios, roughly chopped

Using a sharp paring knife, trim off the tops and bottoms of the oranges. Stand one orange on end and carefully cut the peel and pith from the flesh, following the curve of the fruit from the top to the bottom. Cut each section away from the membranes and place in a large bowl. Squeeze any juice from the membranes into the bowl. Repeat with the remaining orange.

Cut the fennel bulbs in half lengthways and very thinly slice. Add the fennel, chicken, vinegar and oil to the bowl with the orange sections, then gently toss the mixture together.

Coarsely chop some of the fennel fronds. Arrange the salad on a platter, season generously with salt and sprinkle with the pistachios and fronds.

CHERRY TOMATO, CRISPY RADISH and TOASTED BREAD SALAD with SHREDDED ROAST CHICKEN and FRESH HERBS

Make this version of Italian bread salad (or *panzanella*) with the ripest local tomatoes you can get your hands on, and you will see that it is summer in a bowl. The tomatoes are a must, but the other vegetables are flexible. Use celery in place of radish, if you like, or add blanched green beans or boiled or roasted corn, cut off the cob.

Serves 4 to 6

1 small red onion, thinly sliced

140g rustic bread, cut into 2cm cubes

1 small garlic clove

fine sea salt

125ml extra-virgin olive oil

2 tablespoons red wine vinegar

675g cherry tomatoes, halved

1 medium cucumber

4 small or 2 large radishes

300g shredded or sliced roast chicken

20g basil leaves

10g flat-leaf parsley leaves

2 tablespoons capers, preferably salt-packed, rinsed, soaked in cold water for 10 minutes, then rinsed again and finely chopped

flaky coarse sea salt

Preheat the oven to 230°C/Gas Mark 8 with the shelf in the middle. Put the onion in a bowl and cover with the cold water. Swish the water around and rub the slices with your hand. Strain and repeat the process 2 or 3 times, letting the slices soak and changing the water every 10 minutes or so.

Spread out the bread cubes on a baking tray and bake for 6–8 minutes until the edges are crisp and golden. Cool completely.

On a chopping board, use the side of your knife and the blade to alternately chop and gently scrape the garlic and salt together until you have a garlic paste. Put the oil and vinegar in a bowl. Add the garlic paste and whisk to combine.

Peel and cut the cucumber into 1cm cubes. Thinly slice the radishes. Put the cooled bread, tomatoes and a generous pinch of salt in a large bowl and toss to combine, gently pressing the tomatoes a little to release some of the juices.

Drain the onion slices and pat dry well. Place all in a large serving bowl, then add the bread mixture, chicken, basil, parsley and capers. Toss to combine. Whisk the garlic paste dressing together, add to the salad and toss once more. Season with coarse sea salt.

> ### relishing the raw
>
> If uncooked onions send you running, read on. The technique of soaking and rinsing onion takes away the 'raw bite', pulling the vegetable's sweetness to the forefront. Once dressed, the onions become pickled or 'cooked' by the vinegar; they hardly taste raw at all.

RED QUINOA SALAD *with* ROAST CHICKEN, TART APPLE, CRACKED PEPPER *and* FRESH BASIL

Serves 4

Tiny quinoa – what the little grain lacks in size, it more than makes up for with its fresh, nutty flavour and impressive nutritional 'cred'. Deemed a supergrain, quinoa is rich in antioxidants, easy-to-digest fibre and immune-system boosting amino acids; extremely high in protein, wheat-free, gluten-free and quick and easy to cook. Red quinoa is heartier-tasting than white, but both varieties are light and fluffy, and either can be used here.

175g pre-washed red quinoa

300g small shreds roast chicken

1 Granny Smith apple, cut into 3mm slices, then into 2.5cm matchsticks

5g thinly sliced basil leaves

2 spring onions, thinly sliced on a long diagonal

6 tablespoons fresh lemon juice (from 2 lemons)

3 tablespoons extra-virgin olive oil

1 teaspoon fine sea salt

freshly ground black pepper

In a 1.4-litre saucepan, add the quinoa and 475ml and bring to the boil. Reduce to a simmer, cover and cook for about 15 minutes until the water is absorbed. Spread the cooked quinoa on a large plate and leave to cool.

In a large bowl, toss together the cooled quinoa, chicken, apple, basil and spring onions. Add the lemon juice, oil and salt, and toss once more. Season with pepper.

rinsing quinoa

Check your packet of quinoa for preparation instructions. If it has not been fully cleaned and rinsed, they will direct you to rinse well before cooking to remove the off-tasting coating of saponin, which the plant naturally produces to keep birds and insects at bay.

ROAST CHICKEN *and* THICK-SLICED SUMMER TOMATOES *with* SPANISH OLIVE OIL *and* FRESH HERBS

Serves 4

This is the best kind of lazy-summer-day dish. It's ready in minutes and is beautiful, easy and ridiculously satisfying. Any single variety or mix of type, size or shape of tomatoes works – as long as they're fully ripe and, when cut into, brimming with juice. I specify Castillo do Canena, a fruity Spanish extra-virgin olive oil, because it's among my all-time favourites and the one I like best for this recipe, but great olive oil can be had from all sorts of places, and you can use whatever you like.

1 teaspoon whole black peppercorns

12–14 slices roast chicken, white or dark meat or a combination

550–675g tomatoes, in season and preferably local for best quality, thickly sliced

Castillo de Canena extra-virgin olive oil, for drizzling (see Sources, page 172)

a small handful of fresh chives, cut into 4cm lengths

a handful of basil leaves

flaky coarse sea salt

Using a mortar and pestle or the heel of your hand on the flat side of a chef's knife, coarsely crack the peppercorns.

Arrange the chicken and tomatoes on each of 4 plates. Drizzle generously with oil, then sprinkle with the chives, basil, crushed peppercorns and salt.

ROAST CHICKEN SALAD *with* TOASTED WALNUTS, GRAPES *and* CELERY LEAVES

Serves 4

Walnuts, grapes and celery are classic chicken salad companions. To perk up the dish, and to provide a counterpoint to the sweetness of the grapes, I add two types of herbs, plus whole celery leaves, which lend a beautiful and very herby character as well. Try smoked or Marcona almonds (not toasted), pistachios or even peanuts in place of the walnuts, if you like.

115g walnut pieces

200g mayonnaise

finely grated zest plus 4 tablespoons juice from 1–2 lemons (see Box)

cooked chicken from 1 x roasted 1.6–1.8kg bird

3 celery sticks, cut in half lengthways and thinly sliced crossways, plus 20g celery leaves from the inner heart of the bunch

225g seedless red grapes, halved

5g thinly sliced basil leaves

2 large spring onions or 3 small ones, thinly sliced crossways (white and green parts)

3 tablespoons coarsely chopped tarragon

1 tablespoon coarsely ground black pepper, or to taste, if you prefer a finer grind

1½ teaspoons flaky coarse sea salt, or to taste, if you have a finer salt

Heat the oven to 180°C/Gas Mark 4. Spread the nuts on a baking sheet and bake for 8–12 minutes until fragrant and lightly toasted. Leave the nuts to cool, then coarsely chop.

In a large bowl, stir together the mayonnaise and lemon zest and juice. Add the nuts and all the remaining ingredients. Stir to combine well.

easy zesting and juicing

With the help of a simple hand-held citrus reamer or press, you can get 4 tablespoons juice from 1 large juicy lemon. If the lemons on sale are on the small to medium size, buy 2, use the zest from both lemons, then measure the juice. Hand-held Microplane zesters are inexpensive and the quickest and easiest way to zest citrus. They're also terrific for grating cheeses, nutmeg and more.

ROAST CHICKEN SALAD *with* SMOKED PAPRIKA MAYO, SERRANO HAM *and* OLIVES

A few of Spain's most treasured goodies – sweet-salty Serrano ham, smoky paprika and mild, plump, pimiento-stuffed olives – make a heck of a roast chicken salad. Tasty alongside a few leaves of Little Gem lettuce, lightly dressed with sherry vinegar and good Spanish olive oil, both the salad and the dressed greens are terrific as a sandwich, too, between slices of crusty baguette or soft country bread.

Serves 4 to 6

2 large eggs

115g mayonnaise

2 tablespoons fresh lemon juice

½ teaspoon Pimentón de la Vera (see Sources, page 172)

¼ teaspoon plus a good pinch of fine sea salt

coarsely ground black pepper

cooked chicken from 1 x roasted 1.6–1.8kg bird

25 pimiento-stuffed green Spanish olives, roughly chopped

4 tablespoons Marcona almonds, roughly chopped

flaky coarse sea salt

1 medium head Little Gem lettuce, leaves separated

1½ tablespoons good-quality extra-virgin olive oil, Spanish if you like (see Sources, page 172)

1½ tablespoons sherry vinegar

55g thinly sliced Serrano ham or speck

Bring a medium saucepan of water to the boil. Gently lower the eggs into the water and cook for 9 minutes, then drain and run under cold water until cool enough to handle. Shell the eggs and set them aside.

In a large bowl, whisk the mayonnaise, lemon juice, paprika, fine sea salt and generous pinch of pepper together, making sure that any clumps of paprika are blended into the mixture. Add the chicken, olives and 2 tablespoons of the almonds; stir to combine. Adjust the salt and pepper to taste. Transfer the salad to a serving bowl or platter.

Slice the eggs crossways, then place the egg slices on top of the chicken salad and sprinkle with coarse salt, pepper and the remaining almonds.

In a second large bowl, toss the lettuce, oil, vinegar and a generous pinch of coarse salt and pepper together. Serve the chicken salad with the lettuce and ham.

CURRIED CHICKEN SALAD *with* SULTANAS, LIME *and* HONEY

Serves 4

Sultanas, lime and honey create a sweet-tangy chutney flavour that plays nicely with the curry in this Indian-inspired salad. Whether under a tree in the park or around the table in cooler months, I love to serve this dish picnic-style, with good crackers and little gourmet bites from a cheese shop or delicatessen. It's also tasty stuffed into a wholemeal pitta bread, or rolled up in crisp lettuce leaves.

1 tablespoon extra-virgin olive oil

1 medium onion, finely chopped

1 tablespoon finely chopped peeled fresh ginger

1 tablespoon finely chopped garlic

1 tablespoon curry powder

1½ teaspoons fine sea salt

1 teaspoon ground cumin

cooked chicken from 1 x roasted 1.6–1.8kg bird

4½ tablespoons mayonnaise

3½ tablespoons natural yogurt

2 tablespoons fresh lime juice

2 teaspoons mild floral honey, like orange blossom

55g sultanas

good-quality crackers

Gourmet bites (see Box)

Heat the oil in a 30cm frying pan over a medium heat. Add the onion, ginger and garlic and reduce the heat to low. Cook, stirring occasionally, for about 10 minutes until well softened. Add the curry powder, salt and cumin; stir to combine and cook for a further 1 minute. Add the chicken and stir to combine.

Transfer to a large bowl and leave to cool for a few minutes, then add the mayonnaise, yogurt, lime juice and honey; stir to combine.

Stir in the sultanas. Serve with the crackers and gourmet bites.

---

a simple hunt for gourmet bites

Good cheese shops and deli counters are filled with treasures (sold by the pound or jarred) that can be quickly partnered with a simple chicken salad to create an impressive picnic spread. Look for crackers studded with dried olives or flavourful seeds, like fennel or caraway; stuffed grape leaves; roasted red peppers or sweet-hot Peppadews; your favourite olives; and a mix of sweet or spicy pickled okra, green beans, carrots, beetroot, a few cornichons or dill cucumbers.

FRISÉE SALAD *with* ROAST CHICKEN, FRESH FIGS *and* SMOKED ALMONDS

Serves 4

I go a little fig crazy when the plump delicate fruit pops into markets in late spring and then once again in late summer and throughout the autumn. Thinking of the classic figs with prosciutto, my mind made a natural leap to the pairing of the fruit with smoked almonds, which lend a touch of meaty flavour. Any variety of fig, or a mix, works well in this salad.

3 tablespoons finely chopped shallot (1 large)

2½ tablespoons sherry vinegar

flaky coarse sea salt

5 tablespoons extra-virgin olive oil

1 head frisée (about 225g), torn into pieces

225g medium to large shreds roast chicken

8 fresh green and/or purple figs, stems discarded and cut into halves or quarters

freshly cracked black pepper

40g roughly chopped smoked almonds

In a large bowl, combine the shallot, vinegar and ½ teaspoon of salt. Leave to stand for 15 minutes.

Add the oil in a slow, steady stream, whisking constantly to combine.

Add the frisée, roast chicken and a generous pinch of salt to the bowl with the dressing and toss to combine. Arrange the frisée and chicken on individual plates.

Add the figs to the dressing bowl with a generous pinch of salt and pepper and gently toss to coat with any dressing that's left behind. Arrange the figs on the plates and sprinkle the salads with the almonds and a pinch of salt.

HARICOTS VERTS *with* ROAST CHICKEN, CARAMELISED ONIONS *and* CRÈME FRAÎCHE

Serves 4

Crème fraîche, an unctuous, slightly tangy thickened cream, and dark, sweet caramelised onions add indulgence to the act of 'eating your green beans'. I am partial to haricots verts – the slender, French-style green beans – but any string bean can be used here. String beans, like many other vegetables, are sweetest when freshly picked, so buy them fresh and local whenever you can.

good basic kitchen salt, for the water

1½ tablespoons extra-virgin olive oil

½ tablespoon unsalted butter

350g Spanish or yellow onions, halved lengthways, peeled and cut into 5mm slices

flaky coarse sea salt

freshly cracked black pepper

25g pine nuts

450g haricots verts, or other skinny green beans, trimmed

225g large shreds roast chicken

5 tablespoons crème fraîche

Bring a large saucepan of salted water to the boil.

Heat the oil and butter in a 30cm heavy frying pan over a medium-high heat. Add the onions and a pinch of salt and pepper and cook, stirring occasionally and reducing the heat every 10 minutes or so, for 40–45 minutes until the onions are caramelised.

Meanwhile, in a small frying pan, heat the pine nuts over a low heat, shaking the pan back and forth frequently, for 10–12 minutes until the nuts are golden.

Cook the beans in the boiling water, partially covered, for about 7 minutes until just tender. Drain in a colander, then run under cold water until cooled, drain and pat dry well. Transfer to a large bowl. Add the chicken, crème fraîche, two-thirds of the onions and pine nuts to the beans and toss to combine. Using your fingers, crush enough coarse sea salt to make about ¾ teaspoon, add to the salad with a generous sprinkle of pepper and toss once more.

Transfer to a serving plate, scatter the remaining onions over the top and add a second sprinkle of coarse sea salt and pepper to taste.

with or without the chicken

Try this salad, sans bird, as a Christmas side (it can easily be scaled up for a large crowd), then, if you have any leftover salad, you can add shreds of turkey (in place of chicken) for delicious 'day-after' fare.

MIDDLE EASTERN ROAST CHICKEN
and BREAD SALAD

This is *fattoush* – a lively, herby and lemony Lebanese salad. The technique of mashing raw garlic and salt together to form a paste serves several purposes: the salt seasons and mellows the bite of the raw cloves, and the mashing turns the duo into a paste that can be nicely emulsified into a salad dressing. Sumac, the ground dried berries of the sumac tree, offers a tangy flavour and beautiful colour. It's a nice, albeit optional, finishing touch.

Serves 4

1 garlic clove, peeled

¾ teaspoon fine sea salt

125ml fresh lemon juice (from 2 lemons)

3 pitta breads, toasted and torn into small pieces

225g Cos lettuce heart, leaves separated and torn

225g shredded roast chicken (white and/or dark meat, with skin or without)

1 cucumber, peeled, halved lengthways and thinly sliced on the bias

25g finely chopped fresh mint

15g finely chopped flat-leaf parsley

3 spring onions, white and green parts, thinly sliced

90ml extra-virgin olive oil

coarse sea salt

freshly cracked black pepper

Sumac, optional (see Sources, page 172)

On a chopping board, use the side of your knife and the blade to alternately chop and gently scrape the garlic and salt together until you have a garlic paste. Scrape the paste into a large serving bowl, add the lemon juice and whisk together.

Add the pitta, lettuce, chicken, cucumber, mint, parsley and spring onions to the bowl. Drizzle with the oil and toss well to combine. Season with coarse sea salt, pepper and, if using, sumac, and serve immediately.

garlic know-how

Garlic is best (juicy and full-flavoured) when it is fresh and in season (in spring and early summer). Stored garlic, which is what we all buy in the winter months, becomes aggressive in flavour, and the cloves develop a green shoot in the centre. Cut the cloves in half and pull out and discard the shoot to minimise bitterness and pungency.

SOBA NOODLE SALAD *with* ROAST CHICKEN, CUCUMBER, PEANUTS *and* MINT

This is an easy-going salad with clean, cooling flavours. Soba noodles come in many varieties; you'll find some made with 100% buckwheat and others with lotus root, mugwort, wild yam and more. I'm partial to the 100% buckwheat, which has a rich, earthy flavour. You can use whichever you like best, but just be sure to cook soba 'al dente' (using a pasta-cooking method), or prepare them Japanese-style, by bringing a saucepan of water to the boil, adding the noodles and stirring well (to prevent sticking). When the water returns to the boil, 'shock' it by adding 125–150ml cold water, then repeat the process four or five times or until the noodles are cooked through but still firm.

450g dried soba noodles

1 large cucumber

3 tablespoons Asian sesame oil

1¼ teaspoons fine sea salt

300g small shreds roast chicken

2 large spring onions, thinly sliced (white and green parts)

10g coarsely chopped mint leaves

50g coarsely chopped roasted salted peanuts

Shichimi togarashi, *ichimi togarashi*, Aleppo pepper or dried chilli flakes (optional)

Bring a large saucepan of unsalted water to the boil. Add the soba noodles and cook according to the packet instructions, stirring occasionally, until tender.

Meanwhile, cut the cucumber in half lengthways, then remove the seeds and cut crossways into thin slices.

Drain the noodles in a colander and rinse with cold water. Transfer to a large bowl. Add the sesame oil and toss to coat, then add the salt and toss once more. Add the cucumber, chicken, spring onions, mint and peanuts. Toss to combine. Adjust the seasoning, if necessary. Sprinkle with *schichimi togarashi* or other chilli, if you like a little heat.

---

hot stuff

Shichimi togarashi and *ichimi togarashi* are flavourful Japanese spices that you can use to add heat to this or any other dish. *Shichimi* is ground red chilli flecked with mandarin orange peel, sesame seeds, nori and other flavourings, while *ichimi* is unflavoured ground chilli (*ichi* meaning one, for 'one flavour'). You'll find these spices in Asian markets and online. More basic dried chilli flakes can be substituted.

WARM CHICKEN *and* BARLEY SALAD *with* MUSHROOMS, GARLIC *and* HERBS

Toothsome pearl barley with fresh herbs and earthy mushrooms makes a very satisfying, healthy salad. Resist fussing with the mushrooms once they are added to the frying pan so that they brown up well, with nice crisped-up edges.

Serves 4

coarse sea salt

150g pearl barley

60ml plus 3½ tablespoons extra-virgin olive oil

150g shiitake mushrooms, stems discarded, caps halved, if large

225g button mushrooms, stems trimmed, mushrooms halved or quartered, if large

1 large garlic clove, finely chopped

225g large shreds roast chicken

freshly ground black pepper

10g finely chopped flat-leaf parsley

2 tablespoons finely chopped chives

2 tablespoons finely chopped mint

115g rocket, tough stems removed

1 tablespoon red wine vinegar

In a large saucepan, bring 2 litres water to the boil with 1 teaspoon coarse sea salt. Remove from the heat and add the barley, then return, reduce to a low boil and cook the barley for 40–45 minutes until tender yet still firm to the bite.

About 20 minutes before the barley is ready, cook the mushrooms. Heat the 60ml of oil in a 30cm heavy frying pan over a medium-high heat. Add about one-third of the mushrooms and stir once or twice, then cook without stirring for about 3 minutes until the mushrooms begin to brown. Push the mushrooms to the side of the pan, add more mushrooms and cook in the same manner until all the mushrooms are in the frying pan and nicely browned, about 10 minutes in total (if, towards the end, the first handful is browning too much, push them on top of the more newly added). Remove the pan from the heat. Add the garlic, then the chicken and toss to combine. Season with salt and pepper.

Drain the cooked barley and transfer to a large bowl; add 2 tablespoons of the remaining oil, the parsley, chives and mint. Then add the mushroom mixture and stir to combine. Season with salt and pepper.

In a second bowl, toss the rocket with the remaining oil and the vinegar. Season to taste with salt and pepper. Serve the rocket with the warm barley and mushrooms.

Chapter four

ROAST CHICKEN SOUPS

ROAST CHICKEN STOCK

There's no match – in quality or flavour – for homemade stock. It's peerless for making soups, risottos and more; the perfect tonic when you're feeling under the weather; or a satisfying midday snack, sipped from a mug on a chilly day. To make stock, you're using ingredients you might otherwise throw away: a picked-over roast chicken carcass; an odd carrot, celery stick or onion; a stray herb sprig or two. These are the basics, but making stock is an improvisational endeavour. If you like, add a chunk or two of peeled celeriac, a coarsely chopped parsnip, a piece of Parmigiano-Reggiano cheese rind, mushroom stems, a halved tomato or two and/or a couple of whole dried chillies. The longer it slowly simmers, the richer stock becomes – make a light or rich brew; it's up to you. A rich stock can always be stretched with a little water if you don't have enough for a recipe.

Makes 2 to 4 litres

1 or 2 roast chicken carcasses, picked of meat, plus necks, if you have them

1 medium onion, quartered (with skin on)

2–4 gently crushed, unpeeled garlic cloves, or 1 whole head garlic with the top 1cm cut off to expose the cloves if making a larger batch of stock

1–2 carrots, cut lengthways into 5cm pieces

1–2 celery sticks, cut lengthways into 5cm pieces

1 teaspoon whole black peppercorns

a handful of parsley sprigs and/or other fresh herb sprigs, such as rosemary, oregano, marjoram, sage and thyme

Combine all of the ingredients, and as many of the optional ingredients (see above) in a large saucepan and add water to cover by several centimetres. Bring the water to a simmer over a medium heat, then reduce the heat so that you have it is barely simmering (bubbles just breaking the surface of the water) and cook until the stock is reduced and flavourful. This will generally take 2–3 hours for a light stock, or 3–6 hours for a richer stock.

When the broth is ready, pour it through a fine-mesh sieve into a large bowl and discard the solids. If using the broth right away, skim off and discard any fat. If not, cool the broth completely, then chill, covered (it will last for 3 days), and discard any solidified fat. When you use the broth, season it to taste.

> ## using the freezer for roast chicken stock
>
> As you roast chickens, freeze necks, backs and carcasses in resealable bags. Fresh herbs and Parmesan rinds can also be kept frozen for use in soups. Ingredients do not need to be thawed before using. You can make a stock with just 1 carcass, or wait until you have 2 or more for a larger batch. Once made, freeze stock in 475ml-1 litre plastic containers, depending on how you usually use it. Leave 2.5cm of space between the stock and the lid; liquid expands when it freezes. Label and date frozen stock, and use it within 6-8 months.

ROAST CHICKEN SOUP *with* WHEAT BERRIES, PARSNIPS *and* KALE

Serves 4

The chewy bite of hearty wheat berries is nice in soups. The grain is easy to cook and soaks up the flavour of a good – especially homemade – chicken stock. Try mustard greens or turnip tops in place of the kale, if you like. When you want a more complex dish and a little richness and protein, top this soup with a poached egg.

2 litres chicken stock, preferably homemade (see opposite)

125g wheat berries or spelt

2 medium parsnips, peeled, quartered lengthways and cores discarded if woody

225g kale

150g medium shreds roast chicken

coarse sea salt

freshly ground black pepper

¼ lemon, halved

good-quality extra-virgin olive oil, for drizzling

Combine the stock and wheat berries in a large saucepan. Bring to the boil over a high heat. Reduce to a simmer and cook, covered, for about 1 hour until the wheat berries are tender and chewy.

Meanwhile, cut the parsnips into 4mm cubes. Discard the centre ribs of the kale. Cut the leaves crossways into 2.5cm slices.

When the wheat berries are tender, stir in the parsnips, kale and chicken and simmer for 3–5 minutes until the vegetables are just tender. Season with salt and pepper (if you are using unsalted homemade broth, you may need to season with salt generously).

Ladle the soup into bowls, squeeze a little lemon juice over the top of each serving, and drizzle with oil.

cooking healthy grains does not have to slow you down

Getting food to the table quickly is often more about good kitchen organisation than anything else. Wheat berries require about 1 hour's cooking time. Set up your simmering stock and grains first. While the grains are cooking, prepare the parsnips and kale. By the time you set the table and tidy up the kitchen, the soup will be ready for its quick final preparation steps. You can also cook the wheat berries in the stock 1-2 days ahead, and then finish preparing the soup in about 15 minutes, just before serving.

ROAST CHICKEN SOUP
with POTATOES and FENNEL

Serves 4

One chilly February afternoon, my husband Steve and I pulled some chicken, fennel and leftover roasted potatoes from the fridge and in minutes put together this soup, which is now one of our favourites. If you don't already have potatoes roasted, your soup will take a little longer, but not much. The spuds are cut small so that they cook up quickly. I have tried using boiled potatoes here, but the flavour and the starchy quality of the roasted is much better.

350g Pink Fir Apple or other speciality waxy potato

1 tablespoon extra-virgin olive oil

flaky coarse sea salt

1 litre chicken stock, preferably homemade (see page 98)

1 small fennel bulb, cored and cut into 5mm pieces, fronds roughly chopped

225g medium shreds roast chicken

freshly ground black pepper

Preheat the oven to 220°C/Gas Mark 7. Line a baking sheet with baking parchment.

Cut the potatoes in half lengthways, then cut the pieces into halves or quarters, depending on their size. On the prepared baking sheet, toss the potatoes with the oil and ¼ teaspoon of salt. Roast for 15 minutes, then stir. Roast the potatoes for about a further 5 minutes until they are tender. Remove the potatoes from the oven and transfer to a chopping board; leave until cool enough to handle, then cut into bite-sized pieces.

Bring the stock to a simmer in a large saucepan. Add the fennel pieces, return the stock to a simmer and cook for 1 minute, then add the potatoes and chicken. Cook the soup for a further 2 minutes until the fennel is slightly tender yet still retains its texture.

Remove the soup from the heat and season with salt and pepper. Ladle into bowls and top with the fennel fronds.

ROAST CHICKEN NOODLE SOUP
with LEEKS, PEAS *and* DILL

Rings of lightly caramelised leeks give an otherwise simple chicken noodle soup a buttery sweetness and a little visual elegance. Purchase long, skinny leeks rather than the squatter, fatter types, if you have a choice (you'll get more rings), or buy an extra leek. You can use any shape of small pasta or break up larger ones, like pappardelle, to make square-like pieces.

Serves 4 to 6

2 tablespoons extra-virgin olive oil

3 leeks, tough outer leaves discarded, white and very pale green parts cut crossways into 4mm pieces, keeping the rings intact

flaky coarse sea salt

freshly ground black pepper

1.7 litres chicken stock, preferably homemade (see page 98)

1 garlic clove, gently crushed and peeled

175g dried small pasta shapes

450g medium shreds roast chicken

225g frozen peas, thawed

2 tablespoons finely chopped dill

Heat the oil in a 30cm frying pan over a medium–high heat. Add the leeks in a single layer, cut-side down. Reduce the heat to medium–low, season the leeks with a generous pinch of salt and pepper and cook, turning once and reducing the heat to low halfway through, for about 18 minutes until both sides are golden.

Meanwhile, bring the stock and garlic to a boil in a 4.75-litre saucepan, stir in the noodles and cook, stirring occasionally, for 10–12 minutes until tender but still firm to the bite. Remove and discard the garlic.

Set aside a few leeks per serving for garnish. Add the remaining leeks to the soup, along with the chicken, peas and dill, and cook for a further 2 minutes. Season with salt and pepper. Ladle into bowls and garnish with the reserved leeks.

LENTIL SOUP *with* ROAST CHICKEN, SWISS CHARD *and* PARMIGIANO-REGGIANO CHEESE

The shards of Parmigiano-Reggiano that garnish this soup are much more than mere embellishment. The nutty, spicy, salty qualities of the cheese perk up the earthy nature of the lentils and pull together the rest of the flavours in the soup. Look for French or Spanish Pardina, or Italian Castelluccio or colfiorito (both from Umbria) when buying your lentils. These types cook up tender with a rich flavour and a toothsome, not mushy, bite.

Serves 6

3 tablespoons extra-virgin olive oil

1 medium onion, finely chopped

1 medium carrot, finely chopped

1 celery stick, finely chopped

3 garlic cloves, gently crushed and peeled

300g lentils (see above)

1 litre chicken stock, preferably homemade (see page 98)

2½ tablespoons tomato purée

350–450g red Swiss chard

300g small shreds roast chicken

2–3 tablespoons fresh lemon juice

fine sea salt

freshly ground black pepper

125–140g Parmigiano-Reggiano cheese, cut into shards, plus rind (rind optional)

Heat the oil in a 4.75–5.75-litre heavy saucepan or flameproof casserole dish over a medium heat. Add the onion and carrot, reduce the heat to medium-low and cook for about 10 minues until softened. Add the celery and garlic cloves and cook, stirring occasionally, for a further 2–3 minutes, then stir in the lentils. Add the stock, 350ml water, tomato purée and Parmesan rind, if using; increase the heat to medium-high and bring to a simmer, then reduce to a gentle simmer and cook, stirring occasionally, for 40–45 minutes until the lentils are tender yet still a little firm to the bite.

While the lentils are cooking, cut the stems and centre ribs from the Swiss chard, discarding any tough portions, then cut the stems and ribs crossways into 1cm pieces. Coarsely chop the leaves. When the lentils are tender, stir in the chard and chicken, return the soup to a simmer and cook for 5 minutes. Remove and discard the Parmesan rind, if using. Add the lemon juice and ¾ teaspoon of salt, then adjust the salt and pepper to taste. Serve hot, with the cheese sprinkled on top.

MEXICAN CHICKEN SOUP *with* RICE

Serves 4

No fancy flourishes here. This is, simply put, a delicious and satisfying light soup. Save some of the jalapeño seeds, either to sprinkle into the soup as it cooks or over the top when serving, if you like extra spice. A dash or two of hot sauce can also be used.

2 garlic cloves, peeled

fine sea salt

2 litres chicken stock, preferably homemade (see page 98)

100g white long-grain rice

1 small white onion, cut into 5mm dice

1 large jalapeño chilli, halved, deseeded and cut into 5mm dice (seeds can be reserved and added to the soup, if you like it spicy)

225g small shreds roast chicken

2 medium tomatoes, cored and cut into 5mm dice

2 tablespoons coarsely chopped coriander, plus whole sprigs for garnishing

1 avocado, stoned and sliced

2 spring onions, thinly sliced on a long diagonal

1 juicy lime, quartered

On a chopping board, use the flat side of your knife and the blade to alternately chop and gently scrape the garlic and salt together until you have a garlic paste. Put the garlic paste and the stock into 4.75–5.75-litre heavy saucepan and bring to a simmer, then add the rice and simmer for 10 minutes.

Add the onion and chilli and continue to simmer the soup for about 10 minutes until the rice is tender. Add the chicken, tomatoes and coriander and cook for a further 1 minute, then season with salt.

Ladle the soup into bowls and top with the coriander sprigs, avocado, spring onions and a good squeeze of juice from the lime quarters.

LEMON CHICKEN SOUP *with* RICE (AVGOLEMONO)

Serves 4

This classic Greek soup is one of my long-time favourites, and a must for lemon lovers. Light, yet satisfyingly rich, its flavour is a balanced blend of salty citrus tang. Short-grain rice – starchier than long-grain types – thickens the soup and adds to its creamy quality.

1.4 litres chicken stock, preferably homemade (see page 98)

70g arborio or other short-grain rice

3 large eggs

125ml fresh lemon juice (from about 2 lemons)

flaky coarse sea salt

freshly ground black pepper

115g small shreds roast chicken

coarsely chopped dill, fennel fronds or parsley, for garnishing (optional)

Bring the stock to the boil in a 4.75-litre saucepan, stir in the rice and cook, covered, at a gentle simmer, for about 15 minutes until the rice is tender. Remove from the heat and cover to keep warm.

In a medium bowl, beat the eggs, then beat in the lemon juice a little at a time, whisking constantly to combine. Still whisking the egg mixture, slowly add about 60ml of the stock, whisking vigorously to combine. Repeat twice, then add the egg mixture to the pan with the stock, whisking to combine. Season to taste with salt and pepper. Stir in the chicken, ladle the soup into bowls and garnish with dill, fennel fronds or parsley, if you like.

---

to soften the tang (only if desired)...

Avgolemono means 'egg-lemon' in Greek, referring to the two key ingredients of its namesake soup. The intensity of the lemon softens over time, which some may prefer, and you can make this soup a day or two ahead, if you wish, or use a little less lemon. When reheating, do so gently over a low heat, to keep the texture of the soup smooth.

BLACK BEAN and ANCHO CHILE SOUP with ROASTED CHICKEN, CORIANDER and LIME

Serves 4 to 6

When I was 5 years old, my father accepted an opportunity to spend a half-year or so working on an advertising account in Mexico City. The whole family immediately fell in love with the vibrant culture and exotic new tastes of our temporary new home. My mother learned to cook on a comal, the smooth, flat, all-purpose griddle that is used to toast chillies, sear meat and make tortillas. To this day, toasting the chillies to make this soup brings me back to that exciting time, though at home in New York I use a cast iron frying pan for the job (stainless steel works fine, too). Adding a generous squeeze of fresh lime to the dish just before serving is a must. The acid brightens up and pulls together all of the rich flavours within.

450g dried black beans, soaked for 8 hours or overnight, and drained

1.1 litre (just under 2 pints) chicken stock

4 dried ancho chillies

200g finely chopped white onion

3 garlic cloves, crushed and peeled

1 teaspoon dried oregano

fine sea salt

175g shredded roast chicken (white and/or dark meat)

1½ fully cooked, fresh chorizo sausages, very thinly sliced crossways (optional)

2 tablespoons extra-virgin olive oil

4–6 lime wedges (from 1–2 limes)

fresh coriander leaves, for garnishing

1 firm-ripe avocado, peeled, stoned and cubed

Combine the beans, stock and 600ml water in a 4.75–5.75-litre wide, heavy saucepan. Bring to a gentle simmer and cook, partially covered, for 1 hour, adding more water, if necessary, to keep the beans just covered.

Meanwhile, remove the stems from the chillies and discard. Using a knife or kitchen scissors, slit the chillies down the side, then flatten them out as much as possible. Discard the seeds.

Warm a frying pan over a medium heat (avoid letting the pan get too hot, or the chillies will burn and turn bitter). Lightly toast the chillies by pressing them, inside down, on the warmed pan for 3 seconds; turn over and press for about 3 minutes until the inside flesh turns a tobacco brown. Submerge the chillies in a bowl of hot tap water, stirring occasionally, for 30 minutes.

Reserving the soaking water, drain the chillies. In a blender, purée the chillies with 3 tablespoons of the soaking liquid until thick and smooth. Stir the chilli purée, onion, garlic and oregano into the beans, crumbling the oregano between your fingers as you add it to release more of the flavour. Add water to just cover the beans by a 1cm or so. Continue cooking, partially covered, stirring occasionally and adding water, if necessary, to keep beans just covered, for a further 30–45 minutes until the beans are very tender.

Remove and discard the garlic cloves from the soup, then stir in 1½ teaspoons salt. Transfer 350ml of the soup to a blender and purée until smooth. Return the puréed soup to the pan, add the chicken and stir to combine. Adjust the salt to taste.

If using chorizo, heat in a frying pan over a medium–high heat, stirring occasionally, for 1–2 mintues until browned.

Rewarm the soup and ladle into bowls. Squeeze lime over each serving and garnish with the chorizo, if using, coriander and avocado.

GALICIAN-INSPIRED BEANS, GREENS and ROAST CHICKEN SOUP

Serves 4

My dear friend, Alex Raij (a gem of a chef who, with her equally talented husband, Eder Montero, owns two of New York City's most exciting restaurants, Txikito and El Quinto Pino) taught me how to make Cocido Madrileño, a tender pork and chickpea stew from Madrid. Making the stew is wonderfully magical. Soaked chickpeas, a hunk of back bacon, chicken thighs and a meaty ham hock are combined in a pot with aromatics and water and the mixture is slowly simmered. Before long, you have a rich, meaty dish that needs nothing more than a drizzle of good olive oil and some crusty country bread for mopping. This version, similar but Galician in style, shares the unfussy technique and is equally delicious.

280g dried cannellini beans

1 head of garlic

½ teaspoon dried thyme

115g cooked, fresh chorizo

one 85g end piece speck, Serrano ham or proscuitto, cut into 4 pieces

1 medium carrot, peeled and cut crossways into 3 pieces

1 small, unpeeled onion

350g kale

225g medium shreds roast chicken

fine sea salt

good-quality extra-virgin olive oil

flaky coarse sea salt

coarsely ground black pepper

rustic bread, for dipping

In a 5.2–6.75-litre wide, heavy saucepan, combine 2.8 litres water with the beans, garlic and thyme. Soak for 8 hours, or overnight.

Add the chorizo, speck, carrot and onion to the pan and place over a medium heat. Bring the liquid to a simmer and cook, partially covered, for 50 minutes or more until the beans are tender (see Box, page 62).

Meanwhile, cut the centre ribs from the kale and discard. Cut the leaves crossways into 2.5cm slices.

Using a slotted spoon, remove and discard the pieces of speck and the garlic. Remove the chorizo and set aside. Transfer the carrot pieces and the onion to a plate.

When cool enough to handle, peel the onion and combine in a blender with the carrot, 125g of the beans and 125ml of the cooking liquid. Purée until smooth, then return the mixture to the pan and stir to combine.

Thinly slice the chorizo. Add the kale, sliced chorizo and chicken to the pan and stir to combine; stir in 1 teaspoon fine sea salt. Warm the soup over a medium heat, stirring occasionally, for about 5 minutes until the kale is tender. Adjust the salt, if necessary.

Serve the soup with a drizzle of oil, a sprinkle of coarse salt and pepper and some rustic bread for dipping.

CARROT SOUP *with* CHICKEN *and* THYME

A little potato gives this soup its velvety-smooth texture. The carrots are slowly stewed, which coaxes out their sweetness. Pick up fresh-dug types at your farmer's market, whenever possible, to achieve the most vibrant carrot taste.

Serves 4

2 tablespoons extra-virgin olive oil

15g unsalted butter

1 medium white onion, coarsely chopped

675g carrots, peeled and cut crossways into 5mm slices

115g new, or Yukon or Mayan gold potatoes, peeled and cut into 5mm cubes

fine sea salt

1 litre chicken stock, preferably homemade (see page 98)

pinch or two of sugar (optional)

2 teaspoons white peppercorns

150g small shreds roast chicken, at room temperature

1½ teaspoons fresh thyme leaves

1 lemon

Heat the oil and butter in a 5.2–6.75-litre flameproof casserole dish or heavy saucepan over a medium heat until the butter is melted. Add the onion and reduce the heat to low. Cover and cook for about 15 minutes until softened. Stir in the carrots, potatoes and ½ teaspoon of salt and continue cooking, covered, for a further 10 minutes.

Add the stock, increase the heat to medium and bring to a simmer. Gently simmer, uncovered, for 25–30 minutes until the vegetables are tender. Carefully purée the soup in a blender until smooth, then return to the pan, gently reheat and adjust the seasoning, adding a pinch or two of sugar to sweeten the soup if the carrots are not sweet enough.

Using a mortar and pestle or the heel of your hand on the flat side of a chef's knife, coarsely crack the peppercorns. Divide the soup into serving bowls and top each serving with the chicken and thyme leaves. Cut 4 lemon slices and squeeze a little juice into each bowl, then drop the slice in as a garnish. Sprinkle with the crushed peppercorns.

CHICKEN PHO

A homemade stock really shines here, and although you can use a carcass from any bird to make it, consider the tea-brined chicken on page 40 – for both the meat and to make the stock – since its flavours are so complementary. The chillies, bean sprouts and other accompaniments are as much a part of this soup as the noodles, stock and chicken. A good squeeze of fresh lime, which perks up and sharpens the flavours of the dish, is especially key.

1 medium onion, peeled

1 x 7.5cm piece of fresh ginger, quartered and gently bruised with
the flat side of a chef's knife

2 litres chicken stock, preferably homemade (see page 98)

6 whole cloves

4 whole star anise pods

1 x 7.5cm cinnamon stick

350g rice stick noodles

¾ teaspoon Thai fish sauce (see Sources, page 172)

¼ teaspoon granulated sugar

225–300g small or medium shreds roast chicken

2 spring onions, thinly sliced on a long bias (optional)

1–2 bird's eye chillies (optional)

100g beansprouts (optional)

4 lime wedges

fresh mint, basil, or coriander leaves, or a combination

hoisin sauce (see Sources, page 172)

sriracha sauce (see Sources, page 172)

freshly cracked black pepper

Cut two 5mm slices crossways from the onion; reserve the remaining onion. Working with one slice at a time, char the onion and ginger slices by using tongs to hold them over an open burner flame (alternatively, you can char them in a dry, hot cast-iron frying pan or in a griddle pan).

In a large saucepan, combine the charred onion and ginger, stock, cloves, star anise and cinnamon. Bring to a simmer over a medium heat, then gently simmer for about 30 minutes until the stock is infused with spices. Meanwhile, in a shallow baking dish, soak the noodles in cold water for 30 minutes. Remove the stock from the heat and stir in the fish sauce and sugar. Cover to keep warm.

Drain the noodles, then return them to the baking dish, pour boiling water on top and, using tongs, gently agitate for 2 minutes, then drain and divide between 4 bowls. Top each with the chicken. Gently reheat the stock, then ladle it over the chicken and noodles. Top with several or all of the following: paper-thin slices from the reserved onion, the spring onion, chillies and beansprouts. Add a big squeeze of lime, the herbs and black pepper. Pass the hoisin and Sriracha sauces at the table, inviting guests to add each to their liking.

THAI COCONUT SOUP *with* ROAST CHICKEN

If you're unfamiliar with lemongrass, galangal, Asian fish sauce or coconut milk, rest assured, they are relatively easy to find, and a cinch to use. Fresh ginger can be substituted for galangal. Both roots plus the lemongrass infuse chicken stock to form the basis of this soup. Lime juice and fish sauce are added off the heat, just before serving, to keep their flavours vibrant and fresh.

Serves 4 to 6

1 fresh lemongrass stalk, trimmed, discarding the outer layers

1.4 litres chicken stock, preferably homemade (see pge 98)

1 x 7.5cm piece galangal or fresh ginger, halved crossways, then pieces quartered

350g pak choi

200g medium shreds roast chicken, at room temperature

150g shiitake mushrooms, trimmed and caps quartered

1 x 400g can unsweetened coconut milk (see Box)

60ml fresh lime juice

60ml Thai fish sauce

chilli garlic sauce (see Sources, page 172)

fresh coriander sprigs and/or thinly sliced spring onion, for garnishing (optional)

Cut the lemongrass in half lengthways, then bruise the pieces with the side of a chef's knife. Combine the lemongrass, stock and galangal in a 4¾–5¾-litre heavy saucepan. Bring to a simmer and cook for 15–20 minutes until the stock is infused with the spices.

Meanwhile, trim the bottom 3–5mm of the pak choi and separate the leaves. Cut the green leaves from the white stems. Stack the leaves and cut crossways into 2cm strips. Cut the stems into 5mm cubes. Divide the stems, leaves, chicken and mushrooms between serving bowls.

Whisk the coconut milk into the stock. Continue to simmer the soup for a further 15 minutes.

Remove the pan from the heat and, using tongs or a slotted spoon, discard the lemongrass and galangal, then whisk in the lime juice and fish sauce. Ladle the soup over the chicken and vegetables and spoon ½–¾ teaspoon of chilli garlic sauce into each bowl. Garnish with the coriander sprigs and/or spring onion, if desired. Pass around extra chilli garlic sauce at the table.

coconut milk

The coconut milk is likely to be separated when you open the can; just scrape it all into the pan and whisk to combine.

CORDOBAN GAZPACHO *with* SHREDDED ROAST CHICKEN (SALMOREJO)

Serves 4

This thicker than average version of gazpacho comes from Andulucia, in the south of Spain, where it is known as *salmorejo*. Roast chicken, not one of the traditional embellishments, is a nice addition (especially with crisped-up salty skin) if you have some around. Gazpacho is best when tomatoes are at their peak. The flavours of this soup deepen over a few hours and even more so over a day, so make it ahead when you can.

115g rustic bread, cut into 2cm cubes, plus extra for crispy croutons, if desired (see Box)

1.1kg ripe tomatoes

2 garlic cloves, coarsely chopped

½ teaspoon fine sea salt

60ml good-quality extra-virgin olive oil, plus extra for drizzling

2–3 tablespoons good-quality sherry vinegar (see Sources, page 172)

1 x 3mm slice Serrano ham or prosciutto, cut into short matchsticks

75g small shreds roast chicken, at room temperature

50g deseeded and diced cucumber

1 large egg, hard-boiled and finely grated (optional, see Box)

Bring a medium saucepan of water to the boil. Meanwhile, put the bread cubes and 125ml water in a bowl and toss to combine. Leave the mixture to stand for 5 minutes, then squeeze all the excess water from the bread. Discard the water.

Add the tomatoes to the boiling water and cook for 30 seconds. Drain, peel, quarter and deseed. Combine the tomatoes, half the bread, the garlic and salt in a blender and purée until smooth. Add the remaining bread and, with the machine running, add the extra-virgin olive oil in a slow and steady stream. Add 2 tablespoons of vinegar and blend to combine. Adjust the vinegar and salt, if necessary. Chill the soup for at least 3 hours or up to 1 day.

Serve drizzled with good-quality extra-virgin olive oil and topped with the Serrano ham, roast chicken, cucumber and crispy croutons and/or hard-boiled egg, if desired.

a hard-boiled egg and crispy croutons

To hard-boil the egg for this dish, bring a medium saucepan of water to the boil, then lower the egg into the water and cook for 10 minutes. Drain and rinse under cold running water until cool enough to shell. Shell, pat dry with kitchen paper and finely grate into a bowl. The egg can be boiled 1 day ahead and grated up to 4 hours before serving. For crispy croutons, cut rustic bread into 5mm cubes. Heat 1cm olive oil and 1 bread cube in a small frying pan over a medium-high heat until golden, then remove. Add the remaining cubes and fry for about 30 seconds, carefully stirring with a slotted spoon, until golden. Transfer to kitchen paper to drain.

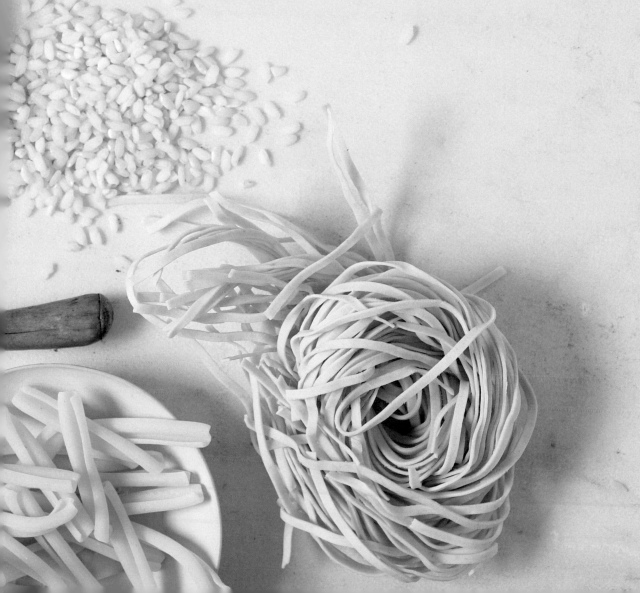

Chapter five

PASTA *and* RICE DISHES

PERCIATELLI *with* SHREDDED ROAST CHICKEN, SWEET ONIONS *and* PANCETTA

Roast chicken is in good company tossed into a pasta with pancetta, breadcrumbs and onions made extra-sweet from a quick oven roast. Perciatelli is a long pasta, like spaghetti, but fatter and with a hollow centre. Bucatini, spaghetti or any other long pasta can also be used.

Serves 4

good basic kitchen salt, for the water

675g onions

8 tablespoons extra-virgin olive oil

flaky coarse sea salt

freshly ground black pepper

225g flat pancetta or bacon, cut crossways into 2cm pieces

1 garlic clove, crushed and peeled

½ teaspoon dried chilli flakes

225g medium shreds roast chicken

450g dried perciatelli or other long pasta

115g freshly grated Parmigiano-Reggiano cheese, plus extra for serving

100g coarse breadcrumbs, ideally made from stale bread (see Box)

10g coarsely chopped flat-leaf parsley

Preheat the oven to 230°C/Gas Mark 8 with the shelf in the middle. Bring a large saucepan of salted water to the boil.

Peel the onions, keeping the root ends intact, then cut into 4mm wedges. On a baking tray, toss together the onions, 2 tablespoons of the oil and a generous pinch of coarse sea salt and pepper. Roast the onions, turning and stirring once halfway through, for about 20 minutes until golden and sweet.

Meanwhile, in a large frying pan, heat 2 tablespoons of the remaining oil and the pancetta over a medium heat, stirring, for about 8 minutes until the edges of the pancetta begin to crisp. Transfer to a large serving bowl.

Return the frying pan to a medium heat. Add the remaining oil, the garlic and chilli flakes. Cook over a medium-low heat for about 3 minutes until the oil is fragrant. Remove from the heat.

Transfer the onions to the frying pan with the garlic and chilli flakes, add the chicken and stir to combine. Transfer to the bowl with the pancetta.

Cook the pasta until al dente, then drain and immediately add to the serving bowl. Toss with the chicken mixture, then add the cheese, breadcrumbs and parsley in 3 additions, tossing between each. Season with coarse sea salt and pepper. Pass round extra cheese at the table.

> ## making breadcrumbs
>
> Homemade breadcrumbs taste worlds better than shop-bought, and they're easy to make. Instead of throwing away stale bread, cut it into 5cm pieces, spread it out on a baking sheet and bake it in a 160°C/Gas Mark 3 oven for about 20 minutes until it's lightly toasted and dried. Leave the bread to cool, then pulse it in a food processor to make coarse or fine crumbs. Store homemade breadcrumbs in an airtight container in the refrigerator for up to 3 days or in the freezer for up to 4 months.

ROAST CHICKEN CACCIATORE
with POLENTA

Serves 4

Cacciatore means 'hunter's style', which is probably more a reference to versions of this dish prepared with rabbit rather than those made with chicken (both are classic). Either way, it's a fresh-tasting, meaty and tomatoey-sweet dish that's delicious over soft, warm polenta.

5 tablespoons extra-virgin olive oil

1 red pepper, thinly sliced

1 medium onion, thinly sliced

4 garlic cloves, thinly sliced

2 x 400g cans whole peeled tomatoes in juice (preferably San Marzano)

fine sea salt

¼ teaspoon dried chilli flakes

375g large shreds roast chicken

225g polenta

Heat the oil in a 5.2-litre flameproof casserole dish or heavy saucepan over a medium-high heat. Add the pepper, onion and garlic, reduce the heat to medium-low and cook, stirring occasionally, for about 10 minutes until softened.

Add the tomatoes and their juices, ½ teaspoon of salt and the chilli flakes and stir to combine well. Bring the mixture to a simmer, then cook, covered, for 30 minutes.

Stir in the chicken and cook, covered, for a further 20 minutes.

Meanwhile, in a medium saucepan, bring 700ml water to the boil with ½ teaspoon salt. Whisking constantly, add the polenta in a slow stream, then cook, stirring frequently with a long-handled wooden spoon, for about 30 minutes until the polenta is tender and very thick.

When the sauce has cooked with the chicken for 20 minutes, uncover and cook for a further 5 minutes. Then remove from the heat and cover to keep warm.

Serve the cacciatore with the polenta.

STROZZAPRETI *with* SPINACH-BASIL PESTO *and* RICOTTA SALATA

Serves 4

Strozzapreti, 'priest strangler' in Italian, is twisty short pasta. Other short types, like farfalle, fusilli, orecchietti and rotelle ('wagon wheels'), work well here, too. The combination of spinach and basil makes for a healthy, bright green pesto, and *ricotta salata* – a fresh-tasting, mildly salty cheese – adds a fresh-tasting and slightly nutty touch.

good basic kitchen salt, for the water

280g bunch of spinach, tough stems discarded

20g packed basil leaves

3 tablespoons pine nuts

1 garlic clove

fine sea salt

6 tablespoons extra-virgin olive oil

450g dried strozzapreti or other short pasta

375g finely shredded roast chicken, at room temperature

good quality extra-virgin olive oil, for drizzling

55g ricotta salata cheese, thinly shaved

Bring a large saucepan of well-salted water to the boil.

In a food processor, combine the spinach, basil, pine nuts, garlic and ½ teaspoon of fine sea salt. With the machine running, add the oil in a slow, steady stream and purée until smooth.

Add the pasta to the boiling water and cook until al dente. Reserving 60ml of the cooking liquid, drain the pasta, then return to the pan off the heat. Immediately add the pesto and chicken, and stir to combine thoroughly. Moisten with 2 tablespoons of the pasta cooking liquid, if desired.

Serve immediately, drizzled with a touch of good oil and topped with the cheese and extra salt to taste.

cleaning your greens

Wash spinach, basil and other greens well before using, since even a touch of sandy grit can take away from, if not ruin, the pleasure of a good dish. A great way to wash is to plug up the sink and fill it with cold water, then plunge in the greens and swish them around. Let the greens sit, undisturbed, for a few minutes, then carefully lift them out of the water, without disturbing the grit, which will have fallen to the bottom of the sink. Drain and rinse out the sink, then repeat as necessary.

FARRO PASTA *with* ROAST CHICKEN, BUTTERNUT SQUASH *and* FRESH OREGANO

Serves 4

Roasted butternut squash pairs best with a hearty pasta, like one made from nutty-tasting farro, which balances its sweet flavour. Pasta made from white or semolina flour doesn't stand up to the task, but you can use wholemeal pasta if the farro type is unavailable. A short curly shape, like torchietti, catches the squash cubes nicely, though any shape will do. Try fresh marjoram in place of oregano, if you like.

1 garlic clove, gently crushed and peeled

8 tablespoons extra-virgin olive oil

1 x 550g butternut squash, peeled, deseeded and cut into 1-cm cubes

flaky coarse sea salt

good basic kitchen salt, for the water

fresh coarsely ground black pepper

3 tablespoons oregano leaves

½ teaspoon dried chilli flakes

450g dried farro torchietti or other short farro or wholemeal pasta (see Sources, page 172)

225g medium shreds roast chicken, at room temperature

5g coarsely chopped flat-leaf parsley

175g freshly grated Parmigianno-Reggiano cheese

Preheat the oven to 230°C/Gas Mark 8 with the shelf in the middle. Line a baking tray with baking parchment.

In a small saucepan, combine the garlic and 7 tablespoons of the oil. Heat just until the oil begins to sizzle, then remove the pan from the heat and set aside.

On the prepared baking tray, toss together the squash cubes, the remaining tablespoon oil and a generous pinch of coarse sea salt and pepper to coat. Roast the squash, stirring once and rotating the tray halfway through, for about 20 minutes until tender and golden.

Meanwhile, bring a large saucepan of salted water to the boil.

Remove the squash from the oven and, while hot, sprinkle with the oregano and chilli flakes, then put the tray on a wire rack.

Cook the pasta in the boiling water until al dente. Meanwhile, discard the garlic clove from the reserved oil. Gently warm the reserved oil over a low heat.

Reserving 2 tablespoons of the cooking liquid, drain the pasta and transfer to a large serving bowl. Add the reserved cooking liquid, warmed oil, squash and herbs, chicken and parsley, and toss to combine. Add 115g of the cheese and toss once more. Serve immediately, sprinkled with the remaining cheese and coarse sea salt and pepper.

PASTA CARBONARA *with* ROAST CHICKEN *and* SUGAR SNAP PEAS

Serves 4

Chicken and sugar snap peas in a carbonara is not classic, but a nice twist on this creamy indulgent dish. The peas are a natural fit for bacon and eggs, and add an attractive touch of green.

good basic kitchen salt, for the water

225g thick-cut smoked bacon or flat pancetta, preferably cut in one 1cm thick slice

100g sugar snap peas, strings discard and cut crossways into 5mm pieces

3 tablespoons extra-virgin olive oil

3 large garlic cloves, gently crushed and peeled

125ml dry white wine

450g dried spaghetti

225g medium shreds roast chicken

3 large eggs, lightly beaten

175g freshly grated Parmigiano-Reggiano cheese

15g finely chopped fresh parsley

2 teaspoons freshly coarsely ground black pepper

Bring a large saucepan of salted water to the boil. If the bacon is 1cm thick cut, cut it crossways into 5mm pieces. If it is thinner, cut it crossways into 2.5cm pieces.

In a medium frying pan, combine the peas, oil and garlic. Cook over a medium heat for about 5 minutes until the oil is warmed and fragrant and the peas are tender yet still have a little snap. Remove the frying pan from the heat. Using a slotted spoon, discard the garlic and transfer the peas to a large serving bowl (big enough to toss the cooked pasta in). Return the pan to a medium–high heat. Add the bacon and cook, stirring occasionally, for about 4 minutes until the edges are crisp, then add the wine and cook for a further 2 minutes. Remove from the heat.

Cook the pasta in the boiling water until al dente. Meanwhile, add the chicken to the frying pan with the bacon and oil, and gently warm.

Add the beaten eggs, 125g of the cheese, the parsley and pepper to the bowl with the peas; whisk to combine.

Drain the pasta and immediately add it to the bowl with the egg mixture, then add the chicken mixture. Quickly and thoroughly toss the pasta to coat the strands well with the sauce. Add the remaining cheese and toss once more. Serve immediately.

buying bacon

If you can purchase the bacon or flat pancetta for this dish from a butcher's or good supermarket meat counter, ask for a 1cm thick piece, then cut the piece crossways into 4mm batons (the batons, once cooked, have salty-crisp edges and a good toothsome bite). Otherwise, use a thick-cut bacon (a little thinner than the first option, but still good) and cut the strips crossways into 2.5cm pieces.

BAKED MACARONI and CHEESE with ROAST CHICKEN, SMOKED MOZZARELLA and ROSEMARY

There are a few steps here and maybe an extra pot or two to clean, but this macaroni cheese is crazy delicious (in other words, totally worth it). Have your onion sliced, cheeses grated, chicken shredded and herbs chopped before going to the hob, and you'll sail right through.

Serves 4 to 6

good basic kitchen salt, for the water

225g dried penne pasta

1 tablespoon extra-virgin olive oil

1 small onion, thinly sliced

fine sea salt

225g smoked mozzarella or scamorza cheese, coarsely grated

225g medium shreds roast chicken

115g finely grated Parmigiano-Reggiano cheese

1 tablespoon finely chopped fresh rosemary

35g unsalted butter, plus extra for greasing

3 tablespoons unbleached plain flour

600ml full-fat milk, heated to a simmer

2 garlic cloves, peeled

freshly ground black pepper

Preheat the oven to 230°C/Gas Mark 8. Grease a 1.4-litre gratin or baking dish.

Bring a large saucepan of salted water to the boil. Add the pasta and cook, stirring occasionally, according to the packet instructions until al dente, then drain and run under cold water. Transfer to a large bowl.

Heat the oil in a frying pan over a medium heat. Add the onion and a pinch of fine sea salt, reduce the heat to medium-low and cook, stirring occasionally, for about 10 minutes until softened and lightly golden.

Add the onion to the pasta and stir to combine, then add the mozzarella, chicken, 75g of the cheese and the rosemary. Stir again.

Melt the butter in a heavy saucepan. Add the flour and cook over a low heat, whisking, for 3 minutes. Add the hot milk in a fast stream, whisking vigorously, and whisk in the garlic cloves and 1½ teaspoons of salt. Bring to a simmer, whisking, then reduce the heat and very gently simmer, whisking occasionally, for about 10 minutes until thickened (the sauce should thickly coat the back of a spoon). Discard the garlic cloves before adding the béchamel to the pasta, along with several generous turns of the pepper mill, and stir to combine.

Transfer to the gratin and smooth the top. Sprinkle with the remaining cheese and more pepper. Bake for 12–15 minutes until bubbling and golden. Leave to stand for 15 minutes before serving.

get the good stuff and grate your own
Always use good-quality Parmigiano-Reggiano cheese, purchase the cheese in a whole block (versus grated) and grate it just before using. Pre-grated options might be convenient, but they greatly compromise flavour and are more expensive to boot.

WHOLEMEAL SPAGHETTI *with* ROAST CHICKEN, SHREDDED BRUSSELS SPROUTS, GARLIC *and* PARMESAN

Serves 4 to 6

Most people who say they don't like brussels sprouts actually love brussels sprouts – they just don't know it yet. The key is proper cooking, which brings out the sweet, buttery goodness of the vegetable (this recipe offers just one of several techniques). Here, the thinner the sprouts are sliced, the more sweet and tender they will be.

good basic kitchen salt, for the water

550g brussels sprouts, discoloured leaves discarded, stems intact

25g unsalted butter

6 tablespoons extra-virgin olive oil, plus extra for drizzling

2 garlic cloves, thinly sliced

450g dried wholemeal spaghetti

225ml chicken stock, preferably homemade (see page 98), heated to a simmer

225g sliced roast chicken

225g freshly grated Parmigiano-Reggiano cheese

freshly ground black pepper

flaky coarse sea salt

Bring a large saucepan of well-salted water to the boil.

Holding each brussels sprout by the stem end, cut into very thin slices using an adjustable-blade slicer or thinly slice with a good sharp knife.

Heat the butter and 2 tablespoons of the oil in a 5.25–6.75-litre flameproof casserole or heavy saucepan over a medium heat until the butter is melted. Add the brussels sprouts and a generous pinch of salt. Reduce the heat to low, cover and cook, stirring frequently, for 5 minutes. Add 60ml water and continue to cook, covered and stirring occasionally, for about a further 15–20 minutes until the sprouts are tender but still firm to the bite.

Meanwhile, heat the garlic and remaining oil in a small frying pan or saucepan over a low heat, swirling the pan occasionally, for 5–6 minutes until fragrant and lightly golden. Remove from the heat. When the sprouts are done, leave them to stand, covered, off the heat.

Cook the pasta in the boiling water until al dente, then, reserving 125ml of the pasta cooking liquid, drain and transfer the pasta to a large serving bowl. Immediately add the sprouts, stock, garlic and oil, and toss together. Add the chicken and 175g of the cheese. Toss together. Add the cooking liquid to moisten, if desired. Serve the pasta immediately, drizzled with extra oil and sprinkled with ample black pepper, the remaining cheese and a little coarse sea salt on top.

smart slicing

To slice any round veggie safely, use an adjustable-blade slicer, with the safety guard, or, using a sharp knife, cut a slice or two to create a flat edge. Put the flat side down on the chopping board too for a stable position so that the vegetable doesn't roll while you cut.

FARROTO *with* ROAST CHICKEN *and* HERBS

I love farroto, a dish cooked like risotto, but with farro in place of rice. Hot stock is added to the grain little by little until it is tender, creamy and deeply flavourful. A conscious eye and stirring as needed are all that's required. For proper cooking, keep the stock covered, and re-simmer it, if necessary, so that it stays hot. You want a tender yet firm to the bite (not overcooked, mushy) farroto. Leaving the finished dish to stand covered for five minutes before serving completes the cooking. Trust the process and the dish will be perfect.

Serves 4

2 tablespoons extra-virgin olive oil, plus extra for drizzling

25g unsalted butter

1 small to medium onion, finely chopped

1 garlic clove, finely chopped

flaky coarse sea salt

400g farro (see Sources, page 172)

125ml dry white wine

1 litre chicken stock, preferably homemade (see page 98), heated to a simmer

½ teaspoon fine sea salt

85g freshly grated Parmigiano-Reggiano cheese, plus extra for serving

225g medium shreds roast chicken (dark and/or white meat)

15g chopped mixed fresh herbs, such as basil, marjoram, parsley, thyme and chives

freshly ground black pepper

Heat the oil and butter in a large, heavy saucepan or flameproof casserole dish over a medium heat until the butter is melted. Add the onion, garlic and a generous pinch of salt. Reduce the heat to low and cook, stirring occasionally, for about 7 minutes until softened (do not brown). Add the farro, stir to coat with the oil mixture and cook, stirring occasionally, for a further 2 minutes.

Add the wine and cook, stirring frequently, for about 5 minutes until evaporated. Then add 125ml of the hot stock and cook, stirring occasionally, until the stock is almost fully evaporated (when the spoon scrapes the bottom of the pan, you should see hardly any liquid, though you do not want the farro to stick to the bottom). Cook this 'low and slow.' Each addition of stock should take about 7 minutes to fully evaporate; reduce the heat if necessary. Continue to add the stock, in 125ml amounts, until the farroto is tender yet still firm to the bite (you should have about 225ml of stock left over), then remove the pan from the heat. Stir in the fine sea salt, cover and leave to stand for 5 minutes.

Stir in the cheese, a third at a time, then stir in the chicken and herbs. Add 75–125ml of the remaining stock to moisten the farroto, then spoon into shallow bowls. Spoon a couple of teaspoons of stock over and around the edges of each serving, drizzle with oil and sprinkle with more cheese, coarse sea salt and pepper.

CHORIZO, PRAWN *and* ROAST CHICKEN PAELLA *with* GREEN OLIVE-PIMENTO AIOLI

Serves 4

Spain's Bomba rice is the best short-grain variety for paella because it absorbs larger quantities of liquid (and so takes on more flavour) while retaining a fluffy and tender yet firm texture once cooked. Certainly worth the splurge. Spoonfuls of lemony aioli add a nice finishing touch.

2 tablespoons extra-virgin olive oil

2 medium onions, finely chopped

115g fully cooked, fresh chorizo sausage, thinly sliced crossways

4 garlic cloves, thinly sliced

425g short-grain rice, preferably Bomba (see Sources, page 172)

1 teaspoon saffron threads

125ml dry white wine

475ml clam juice or stock made from the prawn shells

350ml chicken stock, preferably homemade (see page 98)

175g frozen peas, not thawed

1 x 200g jar roasted sliced pimientos

225g large uncooked prawns, peeled and deveined

250g medium shreds roast chicken

AIOLI

225g mayonnaise

1 large lemon

1 large garlic clove, finely chopped

3 tablespoons finely chopped pimiento-stuffed green olives

fine sea salt

Preheat the oven to 230°C/Gas Mark 8 with the shelf in the lower third of the oven.

Heat the oil in a 33cm paella pan or a 5.25-litre heavy saucepan or flameproof casserole dish over a medium-high heat. Stir in the onions, chorizo and garlic, reduce the heat to medium and cook, stirring occasionally, for about 10 minutes until the onion and garlic are softened.

Stir in the rice and saffron and cook for about 3 minutes until the rice is opaque. Add the wine and cook for about 1 minute until evaporated. Add the clam juice and chicken stock and bring the liquid to a simmer. Remove the pan from heat and stir in the peas and the pimientos and their juices.

If you are not using a paella pan, transfer the rice mixture to a 38 x 25 x 5cm baking dish and cover tightly with foil. Otherwise, cover the paella pan with the lid. Bake the paella for 35 minutes, then stir in the prawns and chicken, and continue to cook, covered, for a further 10 minutes.

To make the aioli, put the mayonnaise into a bowl. Finely zest the lemon into the bowl, holding the zester close so that you capture the flavourful oil that sprays from the lemon as you zest. Squeeze 2 tablespoons of the juice from the lemon and add it to the mayonnaise mixture. Add the garlic and olives and stir together to combine. Season with salt. Serve the paella with the aioli.

CHICKEN JAMBALAYA *with* ANDOUILLE SAUSAGE *and* BACON

Serves 6

I lucked out in countless ways when I met my husband, Steve, not the least of which being that he's a born-and-bred Louisianan, so he knows his po' boys from his pig roasts. It took a few years of marriage before I wandered into Steve's jambalaya territory, and I still call him to the hob when I'm making this spicy dish. Though most jambalayas call for white rice, I prefer the nuttiness of brown.

175g bacon, cut crossways into 2.5cm slices

450g pork andouille sausage, cut crossways into 4mm pieces

1 tablespoon extra-virgin olive oil

2 medium onions, cut into 5mm dice

2 large green peppers, cut into 5mm dice

4 celery sticks, cut crossways into 5mm pieces

4 large garlic cloves, thinly sliced

400g brown basmati rice

2 teaspoons fine sea salt

2 teaspoons paprika, preferably Pimentón de la Vera (see Sources, page 172)

1 teaspoon dried thyme

1 teaspoon freshly ground black pepper

½ teaspoon cayenne pepper

2 x 400g cans whole peeled tomatoes in juice (preferably San Marzano)

750ml chicken stock, preferably homemade (see page 98)

450g medium shreds roast chicken

1 bunch of spring onions (white and green parts), thinly sliced

Combine the bacon, sausage and oil in a 5.25-litre heavy saucepan or flameproof casserole dish and cook over a medium-high heat, stirring occasionally, for about 8 minutes until the bacon is crisp and the sausage is golden. Add the onions, reduce the heat to medium, and cook, stirring occasionally, for about 5 minuts until softened.

Add the peppers, celery and garlic, and cook, stirring occasionally, for about 10 minutes until the vegetables are softened.

Add the rice, salt, paprika, thyme, black pepper and cayenne, and stir well to combine. Cook, stirring frequently, for about 3 minutes until the rice is toasted, then add the tomatoes and their juices, the chicken stock and the chicken. Bring to the boil, then reduce the heat to medium-low and cook, covered, for about 1 hour until the rice is tender and most of the liquid is absorbed.

Remove the pan from the heat and leave to stand, covered, for 10 minutes, then stir in the spring onions.

TOMATO-CHICKPEA MASALA *with* CHICKEN, YOGURT *and* CORIANDER

My husband Steve and I love Indian flavours. When we're pressed for time during the week, this is a favourite quick dinner to make, and simple, because it's mostly made up of storecupboard ingredients. Try it without the chicken, when you want a vegetarian dish.

Serves 6

300g white long-grain rice

fine sea salt

3 tablespoons extra-virgin olive oil

25g unsalted butter

2 medium onions, finely chopped

4 garlic cloves, thinly sliced

2 tablespoons finely chopped fresh ginger

1½ tablespoons garam masala

⅛ teaspoon cayenne pepper

4 x 400g cans whole tomatoes, preferably San Marzano

2 x 425g cans chickpeas, rinsed and drained

175ml coconut milk

1½ teaspoons granulated sugar

200g sliced roast chicken

125ml natural yogurt

5g coarsely chopped coriander

¼ lemon

Bring 700ml water just to the boil in a large, heavy saucepan. Add the rice and ¾ teaspoon of salt, return to the boil, then cover, reduce the heat to low and cook, undisturbed, for about 15 minutes until the water is absorbed and rice is tender.

Meanwhile, heat the oil and butter in a 4.75-litre flameproof casserole dish or heavy saucepan over a medium-low heat until the butter is melted. Add the onions, garlic, ginger, garam masala and cayenne pepper and cook, stirring occasionally, for about 5 minutes until the onion is softened. Add the tomatoes and their juices and the chickpeas. Using a potato masher or the back of a large wooden spoon, mash about half the chickpeas.

Bring the mixture to a simmer and cook, stirring occasionally, for 10 minutes, then stir in the coconut milk, sugar and 1¼ teaspoons of salt, and cook for a further 5 minutes. Adjust the seasoning, if desired. Serve the masala over the rice, with a spoonful of yogurt, a sprinkle of coriander and a squeeze of lemon.

KOREAN RICE BOWL *with* ROAST CHICKEN, SPINACH, CARROTS, COURGETTES, RED CHILLI PASTE *and a* FRIED EGG

This is one of my favourite dishes; it's very clean-tasting and beautiful, and an easy, fun way to make Korean food at home. The vegetables and a fried egg are separately arranged over steaming hot rice. To eat it, you break up the egg and then take bites of each element, either alone or mixed together.

Serves 4

1 tablespoon sesame seeds

good basic kitchen salt, for the water

450g fresh spinach, stems discarded

425g sushi rice, also called pearl rice or Japanese rice (see Sources, page 172)

4 tablespoons plus ½ teaspoon sesame oil

2 large garlic cloves, finely chopped

fine sea salt

2 medium carrots, julienned

1 large courgette, julienned

140g shiitake mushrooms (about 6 large), stems discarded, caps cut into 5mm slices

200g small shreds roast chicken

½ teaspoon soy sauce, plus extra to taste

2 tablespoons extra-virgin olive oil

4 large eggs

425g coarsely chopped kimchi (see Sources, page 172)

2 large spring onions, thinly sliced on a

Toast the sesame seeds in a small frying pan over a medium-low heat, shaking the pan back and forth, for about 3 minutes until the seeds are fragrant and lightly golden. Transfer to a plate.

Bring a large saucepan of salted water to the boil. Add the spinach and cook for 1 minute, then drain. When the spinach is cool enough to handle, using your hands, squeeze all the excess liquid out, then set aside.

Rinse the rice in cold water, then drain. In a large, heavy saucepan, cover the rice with 500ml water and add a generous pinch of salt. Bring to the boil, then cover and cook over a very low heat for 18–20 minutes until the rice is tender and the water is absorbed. (The rice can also be cooked in a rice cooker, using the same proportions of rice and water. Keep the rice hot until you are ready to serve.)

While the rice is cooking, warm 1 tablespoon of the sesame oil in a medium frying pan over a medium heat. Add a quarter of the garlic, reduce the heat to very low and cook, stirring once or twice, for about 30 seconds until fragrant and softened. Add the spinach and a pinch of fine sea salt. Using a wooden spoon to stir and break up the clumps, cook for 1 minute, then transfer to a large plate.

Wipe the frying pan dry with kitchen paper, then add 1 tablespoon of the remaining sesame oil and place over a medium heat. Add a second quarter of the garlic, reduce the heat to very low and cook, stirring, for 30 seconds. Add the carrots and a pinch of fine sea salt, and cook, stirring occasionally, for about 5 minutes until the carrots are tender but still a little firm to the bite. Transfer to the plate with the spinach, keeping the vegetables separate.

long diagonal

gochujang (Korean chilli-soya bean paste) or other Asian chilli paste, and torn sheets of nori, for serving (see Sources, page 172)

---

sushi rice

Sushi rice is a fragrant, sticky short-grain variety. Though sometimes referred to as sweet rice or glutinous rice, it is neither sweet nor glutinous. You may find that using a good rice cooker makes sushi rice easier to cook, but, with just a little practice, you'll see that this version cooked on the hob is not very hard. A bit of the rice may stick to the pot, but that's okay.

Repeat the process above, cooking the courgettes and the mushrooms separately and in the same manner, using the remaining 2 tablespoons of sesame oil, the remaining garlic and a pinch of fine sea salt for each. The mushrooms and the courgettes will require 3–4 minutes each.

In a bowl, toss together the chicken, soy sauce and remaining ½ teaspoon of sesame oil.

When the rice is ready, remove the pan from the heat and leave to stand, covered, for 5–10 minutes.

Break the eggs into a bowl (if you are uncomfortable with your egg-cracking skills, crack each egg into a small bowl, to ensure that the yolks remain unbroken). Heat the olive oil in a 30cm non-stick frying pan over a medium–high heat until it shimmers. Pour in the eggs and cook, undisturbed, until the whites begin to set, then, using a spatula to lift up an edge of the cooked whites to let as much raw egg white as possible flow underneath, cook about a further 2 minutes (the top and yolks will still be very loose, but the heat of the rice will cook any uncooked portions).

Spoon the rice into 4 large shallow bowls. Place 1 fried egg in each bowl, on top of the rice. Arrange the spinach, carrots, courgettes, mushrooms, chicken, kimchi and nori around the edge of each bowl. Spoon about 1 teaspoon *gochujang* into each bowl, then sprinkle with the spring onions and sesame seeds. Pass more *gochujang* and kimchi at the table.

Chapter six

BRUNCH, LUNCH and DINNER

ROASTED CHERRY TOMATO, CHICKEN, CHÈVRE *and* CIABATTA BREAKFAST SANDWICH

Serves 4

I call this a breakfast sandwich, but since eggs are great for lunch and dinner, too, it's really an anytime-of-day affair. Rosemary ciabatta (a soft Italian white bread) is especially tasty here. Plain ciabatta, a nice sourdough or a rustic country loaf works, too.

375g cherry tomatoes (about 25), rinsed and well dried

1 tablespoon extra-virgin olive oil

flaky coarse sea salt

fresh coarsely ground black pepper

½ loaf ciabatta bread, plain or seasoned, cut into 2 (approximately 10 x 10cm) pieces and split

1 tablespoon white vinegar

4 large eggs

good-quality extra-virgin olive oil, for drizzling

280g roast chicken, white or dark meat (about 8 slices)

85g Tomme Verte or other soft goat's cheese

3–4 tablespoons finely chopped chives

Preheat the oven to 230°C/Gas Mark 8 with the shelf in the middle. Line a baking sheet with baking parchment.

Put the tomatoes on the prepared baking tray in a single layer. Drizzle with the oil and sprinkle generously with salt and pepper. Roast for 12–14 minutes until the tomatoes are collapsed and just beginning to blister. Meanwhile, lightly toast or grill the bread.

Combine 4cm of water and the vinegar in a wide, heavy frying pan or saucepan (about 23cm wide) and bring to a simmer. Break 1 egg into a small bowl or cup and slide the egg into the water. Repeat with each remaining egg, spacing them evenly in the saucepan, and poach at a bare simmer until the whites are firm and the yolks are cooked as you like them (2–4 minutes for a yolk that is at varying degrees of runniness). Transfer the cooked eggs to kitchen paper using a slotted spoon.

Remove the tomatoes from the oven. Make sandwiches by putting the pieces of bread onto 4 individual plates and drizzling each with the good-quality oil, then stack with chicken, eggs, tomatoes (reserving any juices from the pan) and cheese. Drizzle the sandwiches once more with the good-quality oil, then spoon any juices from the tomatoes over the top, and sprinkle with the chives, salt and pepper. Serve warm.

---

choice of chèvre

Tomme Verte, a herby and pink peppercorn-seasoned soft, young cheese from Périgord in France gives a great tangy flavour to this sandwich, but you can use any soft goat's cheese you like.

SWEET-POTATO and ROAST CHICKEN HASH with SUNNY-SIDE UP EGGS

~~~~~~

This elemental dish, made with just a few ingredients, but oh so good, is one of my favourite easy weekend breakfasts.

Serves 4

675g sweet potatoes, halved crossways, then cut lengthways into 1cm wedges

5 tablespoons extra-virgin olive oil

½ teaspoon flaky coarse sea salt, plus extra for the eggs

4 spring onions (white and green parts), thinly sliced

1 whole dried red chilli, crumbled, or ¼ teaspoon dried chilli flakes

375g large shreds roast chicken

4 large eggs

freshly ground black pepper

Preheat the oven to 230°C/Gas Mark 8 with the shelf in the middle of the oven.

Heat a baking tray in the oven for 10 minutes. Meanwhile, in a large bowl, stir together the potatoes, 3 tablespoons of the oil and the salt.

Using oven gloves (it's easy to forget that the pan is hot), remove the tray from oven and immediately spread the potatoes and their oil (using a rubber spatula to get all the oil from the bowl onto the tray) in a single layer.

Roast the potatoes for 15 minutes, then, using a metal spatula, loosen, stir and turn the potatoes once. Continue roasting for a further 5 minutes, then sprinkle the spring onions and crumbled chilli over the potatoes, stir once or twice to distribute evenly and continue roasting for about a further 5 minutes until the potatoes are golden and tender.

Remove the tray from the oven, add the chicken and, using the spatula, turn and stir the mixture to combine.

Break the eggs into a bowl (if you are uncomfortable with your egg-cracking skills, crack each egg into a small bowl, to ensure that the yolks remain unbroken). Heat the remaining oil in a 30cm non-stick frying pan over a medium-high heat until it shimmers. Pour in the eggs and cook, undisturbed, until the whites begin to set, then, using a spatula to lift up an edge of the cooked whites to let as much raw egg white as possible flow underneath, cook for about a further 2 minutes (the top and yolks will still be very loose). Season with salt and pepper. Serve the eggs over the hash.

ROAST CHICKEN, SWEETCORN
and POBLANO PEPPER QUESADILLAS

Serves 4

Quesadillas make a fun and easy week-night meal. I serve these with little glasses of El Tesoro blanco tequila over crushed ice with a generous squeeze of fresh lime, but a glass of white wine is equally good, too. When fresh sweetcorn is not in season, use frozen, or leave it out.

1 large poblano chilli

2 tablespoons plus 1½ teaspoons extra-virgin olive oil

2 medium sweetcorn cobs, kernels cut from the cobs

1 medium onion, finely chopped

2 large garlic cloves, thinly sliced

¾ teaspoon fine sea salt

¼ teaspoon ground cumin

8 x 20cm flour tortillas

140g mature Cheddar cheese, coarsely grated

140g Monterey Jack, Gruyère or mozzarella cheese, coarsely grated

250g medium shreds roast chicken

350g grape or baby plum tomatoes, halved

10g coarsely chopped coriander

hot sauce

Preheat the oven to 150°C/Gas Mark 2.

Char the chilli directly over a gas burner set on high, or in a griddle pan over a high heat or under a grill set on high until blackened and blistered on all sides. Transfer to a large bowl and cover tightly with clingfilm; leave to stand for 10 minutes. Peel, deseed and coarsely chop the chilli.

Heat the 2 tablespoons of oil in a large non-stick frying pan over a medium-high heat. Add the chilli, sweetcorn, onion, garlic, salt and cumin, and stir to combine. Reduce the heat to medium and cook for about 8 minutes until softened. Transfer to a bowl. Carefully wipe the pan dry with kitchen paper.

Place 4 tortillas on your work surface. Leaving a 1cm border, sprinkle a quarter of the sweetcorn mixture, a quarter of each cheese, then a quarter of the chicken, tomatoes and coriander on each tortilla. Top each with a second tortilla and press to adhere.

In a large non-stick frying pan, heat 1 teaspoon of the remaining oil over a medium-high heat. Add 1 quesadilla and cook for about 2 minutes per side until the filling is warmed through and the cheese is melted (if sweetcorn kernels fall out from inside the tortillas, remove them from the pan, or they will pop out of the pan). Transfer to a baking tray and put in the oven. Repeat with the remaining quesadillas and the remaining oil.

Cut the quesadillas into quarters. Serve with hot sauce.

for those who like crema

If you like, you can make a *crema*, or loose soured cream sauce, to serve with this dish. Stir together soured cream with fresh lime zest and juice, and salt to taste.

CUBAN RICE *with* CHICKEN

Serves 4

Some say this dish is from Cuba, others claim Spain. Either way, it's one of the best brunches I know. The combination of sweet (from the pan-cooked banana) and savoury (chicken, rice, tomato sauce and egg) may seem unusual, but in fact it works brilliantly. Serve this with a pot of *café con leche*.

200g white long-grain rice

fine sea salt

2 x 400g cans whole peeled tomatoes, preferably San Marzano

1 small garlic clove, peeled

pinch of sugar (optional)

2 tablespoons plus 2 teaspoons extra-virgin olive oil

2 large spring onions, or 4 skinny ones, white and green parts, thinly sliced

½ teaspoon dried oregano

heaped ⅛ teaspoon ground cumin

225g small shreds roast chicken

2 large ripe bananas

4 large eggs

Bring 400–475ml water to the boil in a medium saucepan. Add the rice and ½ teaspoon of salt, then reduce to a gentle simmer, cover and cook for about 15 minutes until the water is absorbed and the rice is tender. Leave the rice to stand, uncovered, for 5 minutes, then fluff with a fork.

Drain the tomatoes, reserving the juices for another use. Combine the tomatoes and garlic in a blender and purée until the salsa is smooth. Add a pinch of sugar to sweeten, if desired.

Heat 1 tablespoon of the oil in a large non-stick frying pan over a medium-high heat. Add the spring onions, oregano and cumin. Reduce the heat to medium and cook, stirring occasionally, for 1 minute, then add the chicken and a pinch of salt, stir well and cook for a further 1 minute. Add to the rice and stir to combine. Adjust the seasoning, then cover to keep warm.

Peel the bananas and cut them in half crossways, then cut the pieces in half lengthways.

Wipe the frying pan dry with kitchen paper, then add the 2 teaspoons of oil and heat over a medium-high heat until hot but not smoking. Add the banana pieces, flat-side down, and cook for 2–3 minutes until browned, then turn and cook for 30 seconds more. Transfer to a plate.

Wipe the pan dry and fry the eggs in the remaining tablespoon of oil.

Spoon the rice onto 4 individual plates and top each with an egg. Serve with the bananas and salsa.

ROAST CHICKEN MELT *with* PARSLEY PESTO, ROASTED RED ONION *and* MATURE CHEDDAR CHEESE

Serves 4

Friends often ask me about uses for leftover fresh herbs. Turning them into pesto is one of the best: of course, to toss with pasta, but an excellent spread for sandwiches, crostini or crackers, too. Add basil or coriander, if you like. This is a 'glass of white wine' type of sandwich – great for lunch or dinner, with a salad alongside.

2 tablespoons pine nuts

3 small to medium red onions, peeled and cut crossways into 5mm slices, rings kept intact

125ml plus 2 tablespoons extra-virgin olive oil

flaky coarse sea salt

fresh coarsely ground black pepper

40g parsley leaves

1 tablespoon fresh lemon juice

1 small garlic clove, peeled

¼ teaspoon fine sea salt

4 x 1cm-thick slices bread from a large rustic boule, grilled or lightly toasted

250g roast chicken slices

175g mature Cheddar cheese, thinly sliced

Preheat the oven to 220°C/Gas Mark 7 with the shelf in the middle. Line a baking tray with baking parchment.

Put the pine nuts into a small frying pan and heat over a low heat, occasionally shaking the pan back and forth, for about 8 minutes until lightly golden. Transfer to a plate.

Put the onions on the prepared baking tray, making sure to keep the rings intact. Drizzle with the 2 tablespoons of oil and season with coarse sea salt and black pepper. Roast for 13–15 minutes until the edges of the onions are golden.

Meanwhile, combine the pine nuts, parsley, remaining oil, lemon juice, 1 tablespoon water, garlic and fine sea salt in the bowl of a food processor and purée until smooth.

Transfer the onions to a wire rack to cool slightly. Set the grill to high.

Arrange the bread slices in a single layer on a baking tray. Spread 1 tablespoon of the pesto onto each slice. Top with the chicken and sprinkle with coarse salt and pepper. Top with half the onion slices, then cover with the cheese, tucking any exposed onion pieces under the cheese to prevent burning. Cook the sandwiches about 10cm from the heat for about 1 minute just until the cheese is bubbling.

Dollop the warm sandwiches with the remaining pesto, top with the remaining onion slices and sprinkle with coarse salt. Serve warm.

ROAST CHICKEN MAYO SANDWICH 3 WAYS

Mayo. People either love it or hate it. If you love it, you are also likely
to have a favourite brand. I'm a Hellmann's girl.

ROAST CHICKEN MAYO BAGUETTE

Serves 4

This is the 'jambon beurre' of chicken sandwiches: incredibly simple,
and perfect just that way.

4 x 15cm-long baguette pieces,
halved lengthways

your favourite mayonnaise

450g roast chicken slices

flaky coarse sea salt

Lightly toast or grill the baguette halves.

Spread the bread with a good slathering of mayonnaise. Layer the
chicken slices on the bottom halves of the baguette and sprinkle with
salt. Cover with the top halves of bread.

ROAST CHICKEN BRIOCHE SANDWICH
with LEMON MAYO *and* BASIL LEAVES

Serves 4

Citrusy mayo and fresh basil leaves give this sandwich a spring-like feel.
Use thinner slices of bread to make a tea sandwich-style version.

175g mayonnaise

2 tablespoons fresh lemon juice

fine sea salt

freshly ground black pepper

450g roast chicken slices

16 large basil leaves, torn (or more leaves,
if small)

8 x 5mm slices brioche

In a bowl, stir together the mayonnaise, lemon juice and a generous
pinch of salt and pepper.

Place 4 slices of bread on 4 individual plates. Add a layer of the chicken,
and basil. Dollop with the mayonnaise, then top with 4 more slices of
the bread.

CHICKEN SANDWICHES
with 'GRIBICHE MAYO'

Traditional *sauce gribiche* (*oui, c'est Français*) is not a mayonnaise, though it shares similar traits. It's made with a hard-cooked egg yolk (not raw) mashed (not whisked) with olive oil. Cooked egg white, capers and herbs are added; it's delicious and typically served with cold fish. Here, it's done as a mayo, yet deconstructed, since it looks prettiest that way.

Serves 4

2 large eggs

1 teaspoon whole black peppercorns

5 tablespoons mayonnaise

7 large cornichons, or more small ones, thinly sliced on a long bias

4 slices good-quality sliced, packaged white bread

4 Little Gem lettuce leaves, or small Iceberg lettuce leaves from the inner heart

160g small to medium shreds roast chicken

2 spring onions, thinly sliced on a long diagonal

flaky coarse sea salt

Bring a medium saucepan of water to the boil. Gently lower the eggs into the water and boil for 10 minutes. Remove from the water and put into a bowl filled with iced cold water; let sit for 2 minutes, then peel. Cut off the ends of the eggs, so that your slices will lay flat, then slice the eggs crossways into 6 slices each (you can eat the ends or tuck them into the sandwiches, as you like – cook's prerogative).

In a pestle and mortar or, using the heel of your hand on the side of a chef's knife, coarsely crack the black peppercorns.

Stir together the mayonnaise and all but 12 slices of the cornichons. Put the bread slices onto four individual plates. Place a lettuce leaf on each slice then divide the mayo mixture among the leaves. Top with the chicken and egg slices, reserved cornichon slices, spring onions, salt and pepper.

MIDDLE EASTERN ROAST CHICKEN PITTA
with HUMMUS *and* CARROT COLESLAW

Serves 4

Rich creamy spreads, tart pickles, heady spices, crunchy salads and often a little meat make up most Middle Eastern pitta sandwiches. The fun is choosing the fillings to stuff inside. So I hope you'll use this recipe as a road map, and vary it as you please. Try *labneh* (Middle Eastern yogurt cheese) mixed with chopped mint leaves; or baba ghanoush, in place of hummus; wilted shredded turnips, rutabaga or kohlrabi instead of carrots. Add tender spinach or rocket, dressed with olive oil and salt, or chopped cucumber, tomato, onion and herbs. Sprinkle on stoned olives, fried or caramelised onions, or cooked lentils. Whatever you do, it's a messy affair, so be sure to have plenty of napkins on hand.

200g carrots, julienned or coarsely shredded

2 tablespoons fresh lemon juice

¾ teaspoon fine sea salt

1 small garlic clove, finely chopped

⅛ teaspoon ground cumin

2 tablespoons extra-virgin olive oil

200g hummus

4 (15cm) wholemeal or white pitta breads, halved

125g medium shreds roast chicken, at room temperature

Persian pickles and/or other pickled vegetables, such as green beans, okra, baby aubergine or turnips, larger pickles cut lengthways into halves or quarters

10g coarsely chopped fresh parsley leaves

spicy pickled peppers, thinly sliced crossways (optional)

hot sauce (optional)

In a bowl, toss together the carrots, lemon juice, salt, garlic and cumin. Let the mixture stand for 10 minutes, then add the oil and stir to combine.

Spread 1½ tablespoons of the hummus into each pitta half, then divide the carrot coleslaw and chicken among the sandwiches. Tuck the pickles and pickled vegetables, if using, into the sandwiches and sprinkle with the parsley. Top with the pickled peppers and drizzle with hot sauce, if desired.

---

a profusion of pickles and pillowy pitta

Delicious pickled vegetables, such as beetroot, turnips, baby aubergine and more, can be purchased at good Middle Eastern food shops or delis (where you will also find high-quality pitta), or try pickled green beans or okra from any good supermarket or speciality food shop.

ROAST CHICKEN BAHN MI *with* PICKLED CABBAGE, CORIANDER *and* CUCUMBER

This zippy Vietnamese sandwich has so much going for it: rich meats; tangy pickled cabbage; spicy chilli sauce; creamy mayo; a vibrant mix of fresh herbs – all packed into a soft baguette. *Bahn mi* is made with various fillings, succulent slow-cooked fatty pork or pork pâté being among the most popular. Roast chicken is a leaner option, though with a thick slab or two of chicken pâté and a slathering of mayo, it's both flavoursome and indulgent.

Serves 4

2 teaspoons whole coriander seeds

60ml plus 2 tablespoons red wine vinegar

1½ tablespoons sugar

¾ teaspoon fine sea salt

300g thinly sliced red cabbage

1 medium red onion, very thinly sliced

2 serrano chillies, seeded and thinly sliced crossways

4 (15cm-long) baguette pieces, halved lengthways

4 to 8 tablespoons mayonnaise

chilli garlic sauce (see Sources, page 172)

350g sliced roast chicken with skin

110g chicken or other loaf-style pâté

½ medium cucumber, peeled, seeded and thinly sliced lengthways

50g fresh coriander leaves

25g fresh mint leaves

2 spring onions, whites and greens thinly sliced

2 tablespoons soy sauce

Put the coriander seeds in a small frying pan. Cook over a low heat, occasionally shaking the pan back and forth, until the seeds are fragrant and lightly toasted, for about 3 minutes. Transfer to a chopping board, and let cool for a few minutes, then press the seeds with the side of a chef's knife to crack.

Combine the cracked seeds, vinegar, sugar and salt in a large bowl; whisk together to combine. Add the cabbage, onion and chillies; toss the vegetables to coat with the vinegar mixture and let stand, stirring occasionally, for 30 minutes.

Drain the pickled cabbage mixture. Pull enough bread from each bread half to leave a 1cm-thick shell. Spread the mayonnaise on the cut sides of the bread. Then dollop with chilli garlic sauce to taste. Top with the chicken, pâté, cucumber, pickled cabbage mixture, coriander and mint leaves and spring onions. Drizzle the soy sauce over the top, then close the sandwiches.

CUBAN ROAST CHICKEN SANDWICHES
with MOJO SAUCE

A citrus sauce spiked with garlic and cumin, mojo makes a great addition to this tasty pressed 'Cuban', made with shreds of roast chicken in place of the classic pork.

Serves 4

1 large garlic clove

¼ teaspoon fine sea salt

60ml fresh orange juice (from 1 juicy orange)

2 tablespoons fresh lime juice

¼ teaspoon freshly ground black pepper

⅛ teaspoon ground cumin

175g small shreds roast chicken, at room temperature

3 teaspoons Dijon mustard

½ long loaf soft Italian bread, cut into quarters crossways and split lengthways, or 4 soft rolls, split lengthways

75g sliced Gruyère

100g sliced ham

110g sour pickles or gherkins, cut crossways into 0.5cm slices

2 tablespoons unsalted butter, melted

On a chopping board, use the flat side of your knife and the blade to alternately chop and gently scrape the garlic and salt together until you have a garlic paste. Transfer to a medium bowl. Add the orange juice, lime juice, pepper and cumin, and whisk the mojo sauce to combine. Add the chicken shreds and mix to combine well.

Spread the mustard on the cut sides of the bottom halves of the bread, then layer the cheese, ham, pickles and chicken. Cover the sandwiches with the bread tops and gently press.

Heat a large cast-iron frying pan over a medium heat. Brush the sandwiches with the melted butter and put into the frying pan; top with a smaller heavy pan. Reduce the heat to low and cook, turning once, until the rolls are crispy on the outside, the meat is warmed through and the cheese is starting to melt, for about 8 minutes.

MOROCCAN CARROT *and* ROAST CHICKEN TART

Makes 1 tart for 4 servings

Squares of this tart match well with martinis, and they also make a nice lunch or a light dinner, with a salad alongside. Harissa is a North African chilli paste, made with garlic, cumin, coriander and caraway. Brands vary in heat, so you may want to add more or less, depending on which you purchase and your taste. You can substitute Aleppo pepper or, in a pinch, cayenne (also hot, but less interesting, I think, than harissa and Aleppo).

325g carrots, peeled

2 tablespoons extra-virgin olive oil

50g thinly sliced onion

1 garlic clove, thinly sliced

200g small shreds roast chicken

fine sea salt

4 teaspoons harissa, or to taste

½ teaspoon ground cumin

3 tablespoons double cream

1 teaspoon fresh lemon juice

1 large egg yolk

1 sheet puff pastry (250g)

6 cured black olives, quartered lengthways

1¼ teaspoons cumin seeds

3 tablespoons crumbled feta cheese

1½ tablespoons finely chopped coriander or parsley

Bring a large pot of salted water to the boil. Add the carrots, partially cover and cook until just tender, 12 to 15 minutes, depending on the size.

Meanwhile, in a 30cm frying pan, heat the oil over a medium-high heat. Add the onion and garlic, reduce the heat to medium-low and cook, stirring occasionally, until softened but not browned, about 7 minutes. Using tongs or a slotted spoon, transfer to a large bowl. Reserve the frying pan.

Drain the carrots and run under cold water to cool, then slice on a long bias into 2mm-thick slices. Put half of the slices into the bowl with the onions, and the other half into the reserved frying pan.

To the carrot-onion mixture, add the chicken and ¼ teaspoon of salt; gently stir to combine. Add harissa to taste.

Sprinkle the ground cumin and ½ teaspoon of salt over the carrots in the frying pan, then heat over a medium-high heat, stirring occasionally to evenly distribute the spices, for 1 minute. Transfer to the bowl of a food processor or a blender, add 2 tablespoons of the cream and the lemon juice and purée until smooth.

Preheat the oven to 200°C/Gas Mark 6 with the rack on the lowest shelf.

Whisk together the remaining tablespoon of cream and egg yolk. On a sheet of baking parchment, roll out the puff pastry to a 25 x 30cm rectangle. Brush with the egg wash, then crimp the edges to form a 0.5–0.75cm border. Prick all over with a fork. Slide with the baking parchment onto a baking tray and freeze for 15 minutes.

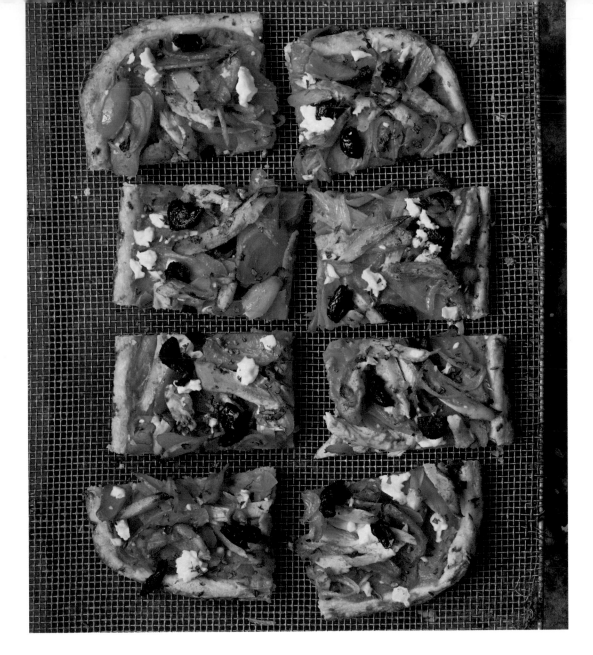

Puff pastry works best when the oven is hot enough to puff it but not so hot that it browns before cooking through. Use an oven thermometer to make sure the temperature inside the appliance matches the dial reading, or modify the dial, if necessary.

Spread the pastry with the carrot purée in an even layer, then freeze for 15 minutes more. Arrange the carrot-chicken mixture over the purée and sprinkle with the olives. Sprinkle the edges of the pastry with the cumin seeds.

Bake until the edges are golden and puffed, 20 to 25 minutes, then sprinkle with the cheese and bake for 5 minutes more.

Let the tart cool on a wire rack. Serve warm or at room temperature, sprinkling with the coriander or parsley just before serving.

ROAST CHICKEN *in* LAVASH *with* TOASTED FENNEL, CORIANDER *and* CUMIN YOGURT

Basic pantry spices, freshly toasted and ground, send a wonderful fragrance wafting through the house and turn Greek yogurt into a bright, creamy dressing for this healthy sandwich. Lavash is a thin, soft Middle Eastern flatbread, similar to a wheat flour tortilla. Look for it in speciality food stores, health food stores and some supermarkets.

Makes 4 sandwiches

1 teaspoon fennel seeds

1 teaspoon coriander seeds

½ teaspoon cumin seeds

175g Greek yogurt

2½ tablespoons finely chopped fresh chives

1½ tablespoons fresh lemon juice

fine sea salt

freshly ground black pepper

200g medium shreds roast chicken, at room temperature

1 medium cucumber, peeled and cut into 2mm-thick slices on a long diagonal

2 radishes, thinly sliced

1 tablespoon extra-virgin olive oil

2 (40–50cm-round) very thin pliable lavash, or 4 (30cm) flour tortillas or wraps

50g fresh coriander leaves

Combine the fennel, coriander and cumin seeds in a small frying pan. Cook over a low heat, occasionally shaking the pan back and forth until the seeds are fragrant and lightly toasted, for about 3 minutes. Transfer the spices to a plate and let cool for a few minutes, then finely grind in a spice grinder or pestle and mortar.

In a medium bowl, whisk together the spice mixture, yogurt, chives, lemon juice, 1 teaspoon of salt and a generous pinch of pepper. Add the chicken shreds and stir to coat with the yogurt sauce.

In a second bowl, toss together the cucumber, radishes, oil and a generous pinch of salt and pepper.

Cut the lavash into four 20 x 20cm squares. Place the squares on a clean work surface. Spread the chicken mixture on the end nearest to you, leaving a 2.5cm border. Top with the cucumber-radish mixture and the coriander. Roll up the lavash and slice crossways into 8 pieces. If using tortillas, spread the chicken mixture in the centre, top with the cucumber-radish mixture and fold up the bottom, left side and right side before rolling away from you.

ROAST CHICKEN *with* RAJAS (POBLANO CHILLIES *and* CREAM)

Creamy, spicy and rich, this delicious Mexican dish is made with crème fraîche rather than the more usual soured cream, which would result in a soupy sauce. If you plan ahead, you can make your own crème fraîche (see Box). Serve this dish with rice, tortillas or both.

Serves 4

1.2kg poblano chillies

3 tablespoons extra-virgin olive oil

200g thinly sliced sweet onions

½ teaspoon fine sea salt

400g crème fraîche

150ml whole milk

⅛ teaspoon ground cumin

375g medium shreds roast chicken

25g coarsely chopped coriander (optional)

---

making crème fraîche

To make 400ml of crème fraîche, combine 400ml double cream (pasteurised, not ultra-pasteurised or sterilised, and without additives), and 2 tablespoons cultured buttermilk in a medium saucepan. Over a low heat, bring the mixture to tepid temperature (not more than 30°C on an instant-read thermometer). Transfer to a clean glass container. Partially cover and let stand at warm room temperature for 8 to 24 hours, or until very thick. Stir well, cover and refrigerate for 24 hours before using. Crème fraîche keeps in the fridge for up to 10 days.

Char the chillies over a gas burner set on high, turning the peppers frequently, until their skins are blackened and blistered on all sides. Alternatively, char the chillies on a griddle set over a high heat or on a hot grill. As they are ready, transfer them to a large bowl and keep tightly covered with clingfilm. When all the peppers are done, let them sit, covered, for 10 minutes.

Preheat the oven to 190°C/Gas Mark 5 with the rack in the middle.

If your skin is sensitive when working with chillies, put on rubber gloves before using your fingers to rub off the chilli skins. Dip your hands into a bowl of water to rinse off the pepper skin bits as you go (do not rinse the peppers, otherwise you'll rinse away a good deal of their flavour along with the skins), then seed the peppers and slice lengthways into 2mm-thick strips. Cut the strips in half crossways.

Heat the oil in a 30cm frying pan over medium–high heat. Add the onions, reduce the heat to medium and cook, stirring frequently, until softened, for about 8 minutes. Stir in all but 100g of the chilli strips. Cover and cook for 5 minutes more, then stir in the salt and remove the frying pan from the heat.

In a blender, combine the reserved chilli strips, crème fraîche, milk and cumin; purée until smooth. If necessary, turn the blender off and use a rubber spatula to stir the mixture and help incorporate the milk. Then continue to purée.

In a large baking dish, layer half the chicken shreds, half the onion mixture and half the sauce. Repeat to make a second layer with the remaining ingredients. Bake until hot, 25 to 30 minutes. Serve warm, sprinkled with coriander, if desired.

3 PITZAS (2 GREEK and 1 LEBANESE)

These Mediterranean pitzas make good cocktail snacks, dinner party appetisers, or a great meal on their own. I recommend using a pizza stone; they are inexpensive, easy to use and produce a crispy crust. A pizza peel is great for rolling out the dough on and, with a little practice, you'll be using it to slide pies right onto the stone.

GREEK PITZA

Leeks, Swiss chard, and currants may not be what you think of when it comes to Greek cuisine but, in fact, they are very typical ingredients and make a lovely pie.

Makes 4 20-cm Greek pitzas

DOUGH

300g unbleached plain flour

1 teaspoon fine sea salt

1 (7g) packet active dry yeast (2¼ teaspoons)

½ teaspoon sugar

60ml extra-virgin olive oil

TOPPING

15g unsalted butter

5½ tablespoons extra-virgin olive oil

2 leeks, white and light green parts only, thinly sliced, thoroughly washed and patted dry

flaky coarse sea salt

1.3kg red Swiss chard (about 1 large bunch)

4 garlic cloves

continued overleaf

To make the dough, whisk together the flour and salt in a large bowl. Put the yeast in a small bowl, add 240ml lukewarm (about 40°C) water, then the sugar. Stir just to combine and let stand until foamy, about 5 minutes. (If the mixture doesn't foam, discard and start over with new yeast.) Make a small well in the flour mixture and add the oil; stir to combine, then add the yeast mixture and, using your hands, mix to form a dough. Transfer the dough to a lightly floured work surface and knead for 5 minutes, then put the dough in a lightly oiled bowl, cover the bowl with a clean tea towel and let sit at a draught-free warm room temperature for 1½ hours.

To make the Greek pitzas, preheat the oven to 260°C/Gas Mark 10 with the rack in the middle and a pizza stone on the rack.

Heat the butter and ½ tablespoon of oil in a small frying pan over a medium heat until the butter is melted. Add the leeks and a pinch of salt, reduce the heat to low and cook, stirring occasionally, until softened and sweet, about 20 minutes.

Meanwhile, cut the stems and centre ribs from the chard, discarding any tough portions, then cut the stems and ribs crossways into 2.5cm pieces. Roughly chop the chard leaves.

Wash the chard and partially spin-dry, leaving some moisture on the leaves for cooking. Heat 1 tablespoon of oil in a Dutch oven or other

2 tablespoons plus 2 teaspoons currants

125g small to medium shreds roast chicken

75g crumbled feta cheese

fresh minced hot chilli or dried
pepper flakes

heavy pot, over a medium heat, just until fragrant, then add the chard. Cover and cook for 1 minute, then stir. Continue to cook, covered, stirring every minute or so, until wilted and tender, 3 to 4 minutes in total. Drain the chard in a colander and let sit until cool enough to handle, then squeeze all of the excess liquid from the chard, finely chop and put into a bowl.

Form ¼ of the dough into a ball, then shape the ball into a disc. On a lightly floured pizza peel, roll out the dough into a 20–22cm round. Leaving a 2.5cm border, spread 1 tablespoon of oil onto the dough. Thinly slice 1 garlic clove and sprinkle on top of the oil, then top with 2 teaspoons currants, then half of the chard and half of the chicken.

Slide the pitza onto the stone and bake until the edges and bottom of the crust are golden, 6 to 8 minutes. Use the peel to remove the pitza from the oven and transfer to a chopping board. Immediately top with a quarter of the leeks and cheese, sprinkle with the chilli and cut into pieces. Repeat with the 3 remaining pitzas.

GREEK PITZA VARIATION

Dried Greek oregano, often sold on its branches in cellophane bags, rather than crumbled into jars, is world's apart from the average supermarket counterpart. I use it for all of my oregano needs.

*Makes 4
20-cm Greek
pitzas*

1 batch dough (page 161)

TOPPING

4 tablespoons extra-virgin olive oil

4 garlic cloves

4 small tomatoes (450g total), thinly sliced crossways

2 small red onions, very thinly sliced

2 teaspoons dried oregano

flaky coarse sea salt

125g small shreds roast chicken

2 teaspoons fresh lemon juice (optional)

Repeat the instructions above for making the dough, heating the oven and pizza stone (heating the stone for at least 20 minutes), dividing the dough and rolling out the dough on a peel.

Leaving a 2.5cm border, spread 1 tablespoon of oil onto the dough. Thinly slice 1 garlic clove and sprinkle on top of the oil, then top with half the tomato, half the onion slices, a sprinkle each of oregano and salt, half the chicken, and a few drops of lemon juice.

Slide the pitza onto the stone and bake until the edges and bottom of the crust are golden, 6 to 8 minutes. Use the peel to remove the pitza from the oven and transfer to a chopping board. Cut into pieces. Repeat with the remaining three pitzas.

LEBANESE PITZA

This is a less labour-intensive affair than either of the two Greeks, yet just as good. Za'atar is a Middle Eastern spice mixture made up of dried herbs, sesame seeds and salt – delicious!

1 batch dough (page 161)

TOPPING

4 tablespoons extra-virgin olive oil

4 garlic cloves

4 teaspoons za'atar

2 small red onions

175g small to medium shreds roast chicken

flaky coarse sea salt

Repeat the instructions on page 161 for making the dough, heating the oven and pizza stone (heating the stone for at least 20 minutes), dividing the dough and rolling out the dough on a peel.

Leaving a 2.5cm border, spread 1 tablespoon of oil onto the dough. Thinly slice 1 garlic clove and sprinkle on top of the oil, then top with ½ teaspoon of za'atar, half the onion slices, half the chicken, an additional ½ teaspoon of za'atar and a sprinkle of coarse sea salt.

Baking one at a time, slide a pitza onto the stone and bake until the edges and bottom of the crust are golden, 6 to 8 minutes. Use the peel to remove the pitza from the oven and transfer to a chopping board. Cut into pieces. Repeat with the remaining pitzas.

ROAST CHICKEN POT PIE
with WINTER VEGETABLES

Serves 6

Most pot pies are prepared with the puff pastry draped over the pie filling, then baked to heat the creamy sauce, meat, vegetables and puff pastry in one go. It looks pretty, but the pastry is often damp and soggy in spots since when laid over the wet filling, then baked, it doesn't have a chance to dry out fully and rise. Here, the pastry is cut and baked separately, which allows it to reach its fullest golden flakiness, then it is stacked with the piping hot filling to serve. If you're not serving 6, you can freeze the pastry you don't need; extra filling can be kept, chilled, in an airtight container for up to 3 days, or frozen for up to 1 month.

12 small to medium pearl onions

40g unsalted butter

750ml chicken stock, preferably homemade

600g total, 1cm cubes mixed root vegetables, such as parsnips, carrots, butternut squash, rutabaga, sweet potato and/or celeriac

50g thick-cut bacon (about 2 slices), cut crossways into 2.5cm pieces

2 garlic cloves, thinly sliced

1 tablespoon finely chopped fresh rosemary

2 tablespoons unbleached plain flour

200g crème fraîche

½ teaspoon fine sea salt

¼ teaspoon freshly ground black pepper

250g medium shreds skinless roast chicken

1 sheet puff pastry (250g)

1 large egg yolk, lightly beaten with a touch of water

flaky coarse sea salt

Preheat the oven to 200°C/Gas Mark 6 with the racks in the middle and lower third. Line a baking tray with baking parchment.

Blanch the onions in a saucepan of boiling water for 1 minute and drain, then cool under running water. Trim the root ends and peel.

In a heavy medium saucepan, melt 15g of butter over a medium heat. Add the onions, reduce the heat to low and cook, stirring occasionally, until lightly golden, for about 3 minutes. Add the stock, bring to a simmer and cook, partially covered, for 7 minutes. Add the root vegetables and continue to simmer, partially covered, until the vegetables are just tender, for about 8 minutes more. Over a bowl, strain the vegetables; reserve the stock. Put the vegetables into a large bowl.

In a medium non-stick frying pan, cook the bacon over a medium heat until lightly golden, for about 5 minutes, then stir in the garlic and rosemary and cook for 1 minute more. Using a slotted spoon, transfer to the bowl with the vegetables; reserve the frying pan.

To the frying pan, add the remaining butter; heat over a medium heat until the butter is melted, then stir in the flour. Reduce the heat to low and cook the flour, stirring constantly, for 3 minutes. Remove the frying pan from the heat, add the crème fraîche and stir to combine. Stir the crème fraîche mixture into the vegetable mixture. Add the chicken, 120ml of the reserved stock, ½ teaspoon of salt and ¼ teaspoon of pepper; stir to combine well, then transfer to a baking dish. Cover tightly with foil.

Unfold the pastry onto a clean, lightly floured work surface. Cut into 12 (6 x 7.5cm) rectangles and transfer to the prepared baking tray. Brush the tops with the egg wash; sprinkle with coarse salt and pepper. Put the puff pastry on the lower rack and the filling on the middle rack.

Bake, rotating the puff pastry once halfway through, until puffed and golden, for about 15 minutes.

Put one pastry rectangle in each serving bowl; top with the filling and a second pastry rectangle. Serve warm.

TORTILLA ESPAÑOLA *with* CHORIZO *and* SHREDDED ROAST CHICKEN

Tortilla Española – comprised of thin potato slices gently simmered in a hot bath of extra-virgin olive oil, then cooked with onion and egg into a thick omelette – is among the most beloved and ubiquitous of Spanish tapas. Eaten at room temperature, tortilla makes for great cocktail, snack or picnic fare, cut into wedges or small squares. A slice on a baguette is also a delicious sandwich. Chorizo and shreds of roast chicken, though uncommon, are tasty additions. A hand-held slicer makes cutting potatoes into thin slices easy, but a good sharp chef's knife will do the trick, too.

Serves 4 as a main course; 8 as tapas

6 tablespoons olive oil

450g Maris Piper or Desiree potatoes, cut crossways into 2mm-thick slices

1 medium onion, finely chopped

fine sea salt

40g fully cooked chorizo, cut into small cubes

6 large eggs

freshly ground black pepper

125g medium shreds roast chicken

In a 22- or 25cm frying pan, heat the oil over a medium heat until hot but not smoking. Add the potatoes and onion. Sprinkle with ½ teaspoon salt, reduce the heat to medium-low, and cook, gently stirring, turning and pressing the mixture occasionally to keep it submerged in the oil, for 20 minutes. Gently stir in the chorizo and continue to cook for 20 minutes more.

Drain the mixture in a colander set over a clean dry bowl (reserve the frying pan). Meanwhile, in a large bowl, lightly beat the eggs.

Beat in 1 tablespoon of the drained oil to the eggs, then add the potato mixture and chicken and gently stir to combine. Add ½ teaspoon of salt and a generous grinding of pepper; gently stir once more.

Add 1 tablespoon of the drained oil to the frying pan and warm over a low heat. Add the potato mixture, spreading the mixture into the pan in an even layer and pressing gently. Cook, covered, until the eggs are almost set, 12 to 15 minutes. Turn off the heat and let the frying pan sit, covered, for 15 minutes.

Uncover the frying pan and, in one quick but careful motion, invert the tortilla onto a large plate. Slide the tortilla back into the frying pan. Cook over a low heat, covered, until the eggs are set, for about 5 minutes more (the centre will still be juicy; take care not to overcook the eggs).

Slide the tortilla back onto the plate and let cool to warm or room temperature. Cut into slices or cubes.

ROAST CHICKEN *and* FRESH HERB SUMMER ROLLS

Like many Vietnamese dishes, these summer rolls, filled with fresh herbs, cucumber and roast chicken, have a refreshing clean taste. If you're new to the technique, don't fret: Once you get a feel for working with the rice-paper rounds, the rolls are fun and easy to make.

Serves 4

1 teaspoon fine sea salt

½ teaspoon ground coriander

75g thinly sliced skinless roast chicken

2 teaspoons hoisin sauce

50g bean thread noodles

1 tablespoons rice vinegar

1 tablespoon plus 1 teaspoon sugar

1 medium cucumber

4 (20cm) rice-paper rounds, plus additional in case some tear

20g fresh mint leaves

20g fresh basil leaves, preferably Thai

4 small or 2 large shiitake mushrooms, stemmed, caps thinly sliced

1 medium carrot, coarsely shredded

4 teaspoons finely chopped roasted and salted peanuts

Sriracha sauce for dipping (see Sources, page 172)

Bring a medium saucepan of salted water to the boil.

Meanwhile, in a small bowl, mix together the salt and coriander. In a second small bowl, mix together ½ teaspoon fine sea salt, the coriander, chicken and hoisin sauce.

Add the noodles to the boiling water and cook until just tender, for about 3 minutes. Drain in a colander, then rinse under cold running water and drain well. Stir together the vinegar, sugar and remaining salt in a large bowl until the sugar is dissolved, then add the noodles and toss to coat.

Peel the cucumber, cut into thirds and then cut each piece into 3mm-thick matchsticks, discarding the seeds.

Fill a shallow baking tin with warm water. Check the rice-paper rounds and use only those that have no holes. Soak 1 round in warm water until pliable, 30 seconds to 1 minute, then carefully transfer to a clean work surface. Blot dry with kitchen paper.

Arrange ¼ of the chicken mixture in a row across the bottom third of the soaked rice paper. Spread a handful of noodles on top of the chicken and arrange ¼ of the mint leaves, ¼ of the basil leaves, ¼ of the cucumber matchsticks, ¼ of the mushrooms, ¼ of the carrot and ¼ of the peanuts, horizontally on top of noodles. Sprinkle with the salt mixture.

Fold the bottom of the rice paper over the filling and begin rolling up tightly, stopping at the halfway point, then fold in the ends and continue rolling. Put the summer roll, seam-side down, on a plate and cover with dampened kitchen paper. Make 3 more rolls in the same manner and serve, whole or halved diagonally, with Sriracha sauce for dipping.

CHINESE ROAST CHICKEN BUNS *with* SPRING ONION *and* SPICY HOISIN SAUCE

Serves 4

Tender meat – often pork, though here, it's chicken – sweet, garlicky hoisin sauce, cooling cucumber and spring onion all tucked into soft pillowy steamed dough; no wonder everyone seems crazy for Chinese buns these days. The Tea-Brined Five-Spice Chicken, page 40, is delicious here. If you're pressed for time, packaged buns, as shown here, can be found in Asian markets.

100g unbleached plain flour

50g self-raising flour

1½ teaspoons active dry yeast

1½ teaspoons sugar

⅛ teaspoon fine sea salt

1 teaspoon vegetable oil, plus more for brushing the dough

375g sliced roast chicken, preferably Tea-Brined Roast Chicken (page 40), white and/or dark meat, preferably with skin

2 tablespoons hoisin sauce (see Sources, page 172)

1 tablespoon Sriracha sauce (see Sources, page 172)

1 medium cucumber, thinly sliced crossways

5 to 6 spring onions, julienned or thinly sliced on a long diagonal (you might have some leftover)

In a large bowl, whisk together the flour, cake flour, yeast, sugar and salt; add 120ml lukewarm (40°C) water and oil. Using your hands, mix and then knead in the bowl until a dough forms (add up to 60ml more water by the tablespoonful, if necessary). Turn out the dough onto a lightly floured work surface and knead until smooth and elastic, about 5 minutes. Put the dough into an oiled bowl, turning the dough to coat it with oil, then cover with a clean tea towel and let rise at a draught-free warm room temperature, until doubled in size, 45 minutes to 1 hour. Meanwhile, cut out 12 (6 x 6cm) squares of baking parchment.

Punch down the dough and form it into a 4cm-thick rope. Cut into 12 equal pieces. Roll each piece into a ball. Place the balls on a baking tray, cover loosely with clingfilm, and let rise at warm room temperature for 30 minutes.

Pat each piece into a long oval, about 12 x 5cm in length, 3mm thick. Brush 1 oval with oil, then fold in half lengthways, place on a parchment square and brush with oil. Place on a baking tray and repeat with the remaining dough pieces. Loosely cover the buns with clingfilm and let rise at a draught-free warm room temperature until nearly doubled in size, about 30 minutes.

Bring a few centimetres of water to a simmer in a saucepan so that the bottom of a steamer insert sits above the water. Arrange the buns, in batches, if necessary, about 1cm apart, on the insert and steam over a medium heat, covered, until the dough is slightly puffed and cooked through, about 10 minutes.

Layer each bun with chicken, hoisin, shiracha, cucumber and spring onion.

SOURCES

ASIAN PRODUCTS

Chilli-garlic sauce, fish sauce, hoisin sauce, sheets of nori, kimchee, lemongrass, fresh ginger, galangal and sushi rice can be found in the Asian sections at most good supermarkets (kimchee will be in the refrigerated section; lemongrass, fresh ginger and galagal will be in produce). *Kochujang* (Korean chilli-soy-bean paste) and products above can be found at Korean markets.

AUSTRALIA

For a comprehensive online directory of organic farmers and food producers and sellers, go to www. organicfooddirectory.com.au.

CAPERS

Salt-packed capers are available at speciality shops, and at www.guidetti. co.uk and www.fratelli-bosco.co.uk.

CHICKEN

'Good birds' can be found at local farmers' markets, good butchers and high-quality supermarkets. For a comprehensive directory, see www. ukfoodonline.com.

CHORIZO AND MORCILLA SAUSAGES

Brindisa (www.brindisa.com) is my go-to source for chorizo and morcilla sausages, as well as Spanish olives oils, vinegars and other fine products from Spain.

DRIED BEANS, GRAINS AND LEGUMES

For Colfiorito lentils, go to www. guidetti.co.uk. Look for Puy lentils at good-quality supermarkets, like Waitrose, www.ocado.com. Spanish pardina lentils can be ordered from Brindisa (www.brindisa.com).

At SeedFest, www.seedfest.co.uk, you can purchase fantastic dried heirloom beans by mail order. Gigante beans can be purchased from Whole Foods (www. wholefoodsmarket.com).

Spelt can be purchased at Waitrose, www.ocado.com; Luigi's (349 Fulham Road, London SW19 9TW; 020 3051 9352; www.luigismailorder.com), which also stocks a fantastic selection of cheeses, olive oils, cured meats, spices and more.

The finest freekeh I know is from Phoenicia Mediterranean Food Hall (020 7267 1267; www.phoeniciafoodhall.co.uk).

DRIED CHILLIES

Look for whole dried chillies at Mexican markets, or order from Mex Grocer (www.mexgrocer.co.uk).

HARRISSA

My favourite brands of harissa, m'hamsa and sundried tomato spread are made by a company called, Les Moulins Mahjoub. Look for the brand at Le Pain Quotidien (www. painquotidien.com).

HERBS

Dried Greek oregano and other high-quality dried herbs, can be purchased at Hambleden Herbs (Rushall Organic Farm, Devizes Road, Rushall, Wiltshire, SN9 6ET; 01980 630721; www.hambledenherbs.com).

M'HAMSA

See Harissa

NUTS

Purchase Marcona almonds at Brindisa, www.brindisa.com; or Café Garcia (246-248-250 Portobello Road, London W11 1LL; 020 7221 6119; www.garciafoods.co.uk).

OLIVES AND OLIVE OILS

Look for Lucques and Cerignola olives at specialty food shops, or order them from Waitrose (www.ocado.com). For a terrific selection of estate-bottled extra-virgin olive oils from Italy, look to www.guidetti.co.uk. Fantastic Spanish olives and olive oils, including Castillo de Canena, and other fine products from Spain, can be found at Brindisa (www.brindisa.com) or online at www.delicioso.co.uk.

PASTA

My favourite dried pasta is Pasta Setaro. An extensive line of the product, as well as high-quality farro and wholemeal pastas can be found online at www.buonitalia.com.

POTS, PANS AND TOOLS

I rely heavily on Le Creuset (www.lecreuset.co.uk) enamelled cast iron gratin dishes, grill pans and Dutch ovens, for cooking chicken and more.

Berndes makes fantastic nonstick frying pans. I recommend the 'Tradition' line, which is made using vacuum-pressured casting. These pans heat well and evenly; the coating does not chip or peel. With wooden handles wrapped in foil, the pans can be used in the oven. Look for them on Amazon (www.amazon.com).

Shop Lodge (www.lodgemfg.com) for cast iron frying pans.

Joyce Chen Scissors are invaluable for cutting the backbone out of a chicken, snipping herbs and more. Look for them on Amazon (www.amazon.com).

RICE

Sushi rice can be purchased at good supermarkets, Asian markets and Amazon (www.amazon.com).

Bomba and Calasparra rices can be purchased at Brindisa (www.brindisa.com) and online at www.delicioso.co.uk.

SALT

Fantastic fine and flaky coarse sea salts can be purchased from Anglesey Sea Salt Company, the only UK salt to be awarded Soil Association Certified Product Status (Brynsiencyn,

Isle of Anglesey, Wales, LL61 6TQ, 01248 430 871; www.seasalt.co.uk). Among my favourite salts are Big Tree Farms Coarse Hollow Pyramids and Fine Grain (Fleur de Sel); both can be purchased from Amazon (www.amazon.com).

SPICES

Aleppo pepper, sumac and za'atar, as well as aromatic black peppercorns and other high-quality spices can be purchased at The Spice Shop (1 Blenheim Crescent, W11 2EE; 020 7221 4448; www.thespiceshop.com) For Pimentón de la Vera, look online at www.flavoursofspain.co.uk.

SUN-DRIED TOMATO SPREAD

See Harissa

BEAUTIFUL THINGS AND GOOD KITCHENWARE THAT APPEAR IN THIS BOOK
(Credits and Where to Find Them)

Ochre (www.ochrestore.com)
Page 42: Linen surface; Page 80: Bowl
Page 124: Bowls; Page 136: All dishes, except empty bowl; Page 168: Small bowl

Le Creuset (www.lecreuset.co.uk)
Page 56: Oval French Oven, 5-quart
Page 98: Stockpot, 8-quart
Page 34: Oval Au Gratin, 3-quart

INDEX

ACKNOWLEDGEMENTS

Much time, effort, and attention were poured into this book, and muscle from many people was applied. I am thrilled and deeply appreciative. Thank you to Anja Schmidt, my stalwart and resourceful editor, whose creativity, spirited nature and keen juggling skills added to the fun and ensured that our ambitious schedule stayed on track; and to Kyle Cathie, for bringing me into an exciting family of authors and beautiful books, and for keeping watch over the UK edition of this one.

To David Black, my exuberant and focused agent: thank you for terrific guidance, encouragement and care; and to your excellent staff, Antonella Iannarino, Gary Morris and David Larabell, for support and loads of help.

Endless thanks to a warm, wonderful and crazy-talented visual team: photographer, Ellen Silverman, prop stylists, Bette Blau and Deborah Williams, food stylists, Anne Disrude and Rebecca Jurkevich, and photography assistant, Kevin Norris, whose vision, thoughtfulness, and tireless work brought real beauty to these pages; to designer, Carl Hodson, for putting words and pictures together in such a perfect way, and production directors, Gemma John and Lisa Pinnell.

To my dear friend, Robin Insley, who connected me to the generous and enormously helpful Steve Gold of Murray's Chickens; thank you both for gorgeous and delicious birds, and for sharing your insight and information regarding all things chicken. Thanks, too, to Steve Ventrone and Jose Vasquez, at London Meat Co., for help with poultry pick ups.

The exceptional support I receive from friends and colleagues – talented creatives in this field and others – is invaluable. Thank you to Jennifer Aaronson, Lisa Amand, Tanya and Alf Bishai, Josh Dake, Karen DeMasco, Stefan Forbes, G. Giraldo, David and Butch Krutchik, Gabrielle Langholtz, Irene Hamburger, Marisa Huff, Bill Hutchinson, Sara Jenkins, Alison Tozzi Liu, Sioux Logan, Julie Miller, Paul Molakides, Jocelyn Morse-Farmerie, Raquel Pelzel, Corina Quinn, Alex Raij, Amie Rogosin Ruditz, Gail Simmons, Jon and Michelle Tate, Michael Wilson, Tia Wou and Amy Zavatto, as well as families Kaminsky, Hoffman, Steinmetz, Sambursky, Rudley and Brown.

To recipe testers, readers and treasured friends old and new, Linsey Herman, Jess Kapadia, Cameron Kane, and Meeghan Truelove: enormous thanks for your generosity and thoughtful help.

Thank you to my jubilant and organised assistant, Sasha Stoecklein, who is a true pleasure to work with and offers boundless energy and dedication; and Deanna Silva at The Institute of Culinary Education, for making a terrific match.

Deepest thanks to my parents, Neil and Phyllis Fox, for fostering my vision of the world through the food lens, and passing on the significance and joy of breaking bread with friends and family; to my brother, Jason Fox, a talented chef, forager and wine guy with whom it is endless fun to enjoy our parallel careers; and to my husband and best friend, Stephen Hoffman, for believing in and sharing every bite and so much more.